NOVELL'S

GroupWise® 5.5 User's Handbook

NOVELL'S

GroupWise® 5.5
User's Handbook

SHAWN B. ROGERS
RICHARD H. MCTAGUE

Novell Press, San Jose

Novell's GroupWise® 5.5 User's Handbook

Published by

Novell Press

2180 Fortune Drive

San Jose, CA 95131

Library of Congress Catalog Card No.: 98-71853

ISBN: 0-7645-4552-3

Printed in the United States of America

10 9 8 7 6

1P/QX/RS/ZY/IN

Distributed in the United States by IDG Books Worldwide, Inc.

Distributed by Macmillan Canada for Canada; by Transworld Publishers Limited in the United Kingdom; by IDG Norge Books for Norway; by IDG Sweden Books for Sweden; by Woodslane Pty. Ltd. for Australia; by Woodslane (NZ) Ltd. for New Zealand; by Addison Wesley Longman Singapore Pte Ltd. for Singapore, Malaysia, Thailand, and Indonesia; by Norma Comunicaciones S.A. for Colombia; by Intersoft for South Africa; by International Thomson Publishing for Germany, Austria and Switzerland; by Distribuidora Cuspide for Argentina; by Livraria Cultura for Brazil; by Ediciencia S.A. for Ecuador; by Ediciones ZETA S.C.R. Ltda. for Peru; by WS Computer Publishing Corporation, Inc., for the Philippines; by Contemporanea de Ediciones for Venezuela; by Express Computer Distributors for the Caribbean and West Indies; by Micronesia Media Distributor, Inc. for Micronesia; by Grupo Editorial Norma S.A. for Guatemala; by Chips Computadoras S.A. de C.V. for Mexico; by Editorial Norma de Panama S.A. for Panama; by Wouters Import for Belgium; by American Bookshops for Finland. Authorized Sales Agent: Anthony Rudkin Associates for the Middle East and North Africa.

For general information on IDG Books Worldwide's books in the U.S., please call our Consumer Customer Service department at 800-762-2974. For reseller information, including discounts and premium sales, please call our Reseller Customer Service department at 800-434-3422.

For information on where to purchase IDG Books Worldwide's books outside the U.S., please contact our International Sales department at 317-596-5530 or fax 317-596-5692.

For information on foreign language translations, please contact our Foreign & Subsidiary Rights department at 650-655-3021 or fax 650-655-3281.

For sales inquiries and special prices for bulk quantities, please contact our Sales department at 650-655-3200 or write to the address above.

For information on using IDG Books Worldwide's books in the classroom or for ordering examination copies, please contact our Educational Sales department at 800-434-2086 or fax 317-596-5499.

For press review copies, author interviews, or other publicity information, please contact our Public Relations department at 650-655-3000 or fax 650-655-3299.

For authorization to photocopy items for corporate, personal, or educational use, please contact Copyright Clearance Center, 222 Rosewood Drive, Danvers, MA 01923, or fax 978-750-4470.

Welcome to Novell Press

Novell Press, the world's leading provider of networking books, is the premier source for the most timely and useful information in the networking industry. Novell Press books cover fundamental networking issues as they emerge — from today's Novell and third-party products to the concepts and strategies that will guide the industry's future. The result is a broad spectrum of titles for the benefit of those involved in networking at any level: end user, department administrator, developer, systems manager, or network architect.

Novell Press books are written by experts with the full participation of Novell's technical, managerial, and marketing staff. The books are exhaustively reviewed by Novell's own technicians and are published only on the basis of final released software, never on prereleased versions.

Novell Press at IDG Books Worldwide is an exciting partnership between two companies at the forefront of the knowledge and communications revolution. The Press is implementing an ambitious publishing program to develop new networking titles centered on the current version of NetWare, GroupWise, BorderManager, ManageWise, and networking integration products.

Novell Press books are translated into several languages and sold throughout the world.

Marcy Shanti, Program Manager
Novell Press, Novell, Inc.

Novell Press

Novell Program Manager
Marcy Shanti

Administrator
Diana Aviles

IDG Books Worldwide

Acquisitions Editor
Jim Sumser

Development Editor
Stefan Grünwedel

Copy Editor
Nicole Fountain

Technical Editor
Howard Tayler

Prodject Coordinator
Ritchie Durdin

**Graphics and
Production Specialists**
Linda Marousek
Hector Mendoza
E. A. Pauw

Quality Control Specialists
Mick Arellano
Mark Schumann

Proofreader
Nancy L. Reinhardt

Indexer
C² Editorial Services

About the Authors

Shawn B. Rogers, CNE and CNI, is the author of *Novell's GroupWise 5 Administrator's Guide,* and *Novell's GroupWise 5 User's Handbook.* He is a product training specialist for Compaq Computer Corporation in Houston, Texas, and was formerly a senior instructional designer for Novell Education. He has six years' teaching and technical instructional design experience with GroupWise and other computing technologies.

Richard H. McTague, CNE and CNI, is an enterprise messaging consultant for Cost Management Systems, Inc. He is the coauthor of *Novell's GroupWise 5 Administrator's Guide* and *Novell's GroupWise 5 User's Handbook.* He has also written articles for *Computer User* and *Computing Canada* magazines.

Preface

Welcome to Novell GroupWise 5.5! GroupWise 5.5 is Novell's newest version of the most powerful electronic messaging system in the world, and *Novell's GroupWise 5.5 User's Handbook* guides you through it. Our goal is to make you productive with GroupWise as quickly as possible. To that end, we cover the most important features of GroupWise 5.5 and focus exclusively on the Windows 95 client.

For beginning computer users, this book serves as a guide to get you up and running with GroupWise 5.5 in minimal time. For more advanced computer users, *Novell's GroupWise 5.5 User's Handbook* serves as a quick-reference for getting the most out of GroupWise's advanced features.

Keep this book next to the computer where you have GroupWise installed. We provide illustrations of actual GroupWise screens and step-by-step procedures to help you learn the system immediately.

The book is organized as follows.

Chapter 1: Introduction to GroupWise 5.5

We set out to accomplish two things in this chapter. First, we explain exactly what GroupWise 5.5 does and how you can use it to increase your productivity. Second, we explain the GroupWise 5.5 interface. At first glance, the GroupWise interface seems almost too simple to contain all the information it does. When you finish this chapter, you will understand how the interface works and how to navigate through GroupWise 5.5.

Chapter 2: Messaging Fundamentals

Here we explain how to use each of the GroupWise 5.5 message types and how to send and receive messages. We give step-by-step instructions for sending messages and attaching files to them. We also explain how to read incoming messages, view and save file attachments, print messages, reply to and forward messages, and delete messages.

Chapter 3: Using the GroupWise Address Book

The GroupWise Address Book is a powerful and useful component of GroupWise 5.5. In this chapter we explain how to use the Address Book to find the addresses of other GroupWise users and how to use the Address Book to send messages to groups of users.

The Address Book can also be used as a personal contact manager. We explain how to create personal contact lists (known as personal address books) and how to add contact records to personal address books.

Chapter 4: Message Management

As you start using GroupWise 5.5 for everyday work, you will soon experience message overload. Just as your work desk can quickly become cluttered with messages, notes, mail, and paperwork, your GroupWise 5.5 Mailbox will quickly become unwieldy unless you practice good message management.

In this chapter we explain how to use the GroupWise 5.5 message management features to prevent overload. We show you how to find out whether someone has opened a message you sent, and how to retract a message when you realize you forgot to attach a file or you forgot to spell-check a message you just sent to the CEO.

We also show you how to set up folders to organize your messages and how to rid yourself of useless messages permanently.

Chapter 5: Personal Calendaring and Task Management

Once you have figured out how to send, receive, and manage your Group-Wise 5.5 messages, you are ready to get going with the main feature that sets GroupWise 5.5 apart from most other groupware systems available today — the Calendar.

In this chapter we show you how you can use GroupWise 5.5 to replace your day planner. We explain how to use the Calendar to manage your personal appointments and tasks, and even how to create notes to remind you about the events of the day.

Chapter 6: Group Calendaring and Task Management

Once you have mastered the art of maintaining your personal notes, tasks, and appointments in GroupWise, you are ready to begin sending them to other GroupWise users. We show you how to do this easily in this chapter.

We also explain how to use the powerful Busy Search feature to access other users' Calendars quickly and efficiently and find out when people are available for meetings. Finally, we explain how to accept, decline, and delegate appointments and tasks you receive in your Mailbox.

Chapter 7: Advanced Features

This chapter delves into some more complex GroupWise 5.5 features, such as rules, proxies, and discussions (online chat sessions with other GroupWise users).

Rules are used to automate many of the tasks that you commonly perform in GroupWise 5.5. For example, you can use rules to reply to certain messages or move specific messages to a folder automatically.

The Proxy feature enables you to set up GroupWise so that other people can view your Calendar and your messages. You can even give others the power to send messages in your name.

Discussions enable information to be shared across your organization, much like an electronic bulletin board system.

Chapter 8: Document Management

GroupWise Document Management Services (DMS) is cutting-edge technology, tightly integrated with the GroupWise messaging system. Using GroupWise DMS, you can manage your documents through the GroupWise interface and share documents with other GroupWise users easily.

This chapter explains how to import documents into GroupWise libraries, create new documents in a library, work with documents in a library, and share documents with other users.

Chapter 9: Remote Mode

GroupWise 5.5's Remote Mode enables you to dial in to the main GroupWise system from home or while traveling (assuming that your system has been configured to support remote GroupWise access). You can use GroupWise 5.5 Remote to send messages to others and to receive messages that have been sent to you.

We explain how to use GroupWise Remote to connect to the main GroupWise 5.5 system through a modem and how to minimize the amount of time you are connected so that you don't run up huge phone bills. We also explain how to use the Hit the Road feature to keep your Remote Mailbox (on your hard drive) synchronized with your Master Mailbox in the main GroupWise system.

Chapter 10: Customizing GroupWise

To round out the book, we explain how to make GroupWise 5.5 fit your personal work style by setting default options, customizing tool bars, and setting folder options. We also give you instructions for setting a password that will prevent someone from hacking into your GroupWise 5.5 Mailbox.

Appendixes

Appendixes A through C cover GroupWise startup, online help, and Internet features, respectively. Appendix D features a convenient worksheet for you to record the necessary configuration information to access Remote Mode. Appendix E provides an overview of the GroupWise 5 WebAccess Client.

Acknowledgments

I would like to thank Kellie and Cameron again for the sacrifices they have made throughout all my authoring projects, and also for their love and patience with me because of the life-changing events my career has put them through in the past year.

Thanks also to my coauthor and good friend, Rick McTague, for sharing his talents, for his enthusiasm, and for doing more than his fair share with this book and our other books. Thanks also to his wonderful family for supporting him in these projects.

— *Shawn B. Rogers*

First of all, I would like to thank my wife, Alison, for all of her support, love, and amazing patience during this project, and also my sons, Richard, Patrick, and James, for understanding why Daddy was in the basement so many nights!

I'd like to thank my mom and dad, my sister Patty, Gavin, my brother Scott and his family, and my parents-in-law, Mom and Dad Turner. I attribute any success I have had to all of my family. I love you all!

Thanks also to Mike and Lisa Strange, Chris and Tracy Carspecken, Paul Palmer, Doug and Bob Turner, Rick and Rhonda Stock, and all of our neighbors and other friends for all their help and support.

A special thanks goes to Stefan Grünwedel and Nicole Fountain at IDG Books Worldwide, who brought our efforts together and made us readable.

Finally, no acknowledgment would be complete without a tip of the golf cap to my steady and faithful partner, Shawn Rogers. I value tremendously, and do not take for granted, our deep friendship. Thanks to your family, and thanks to you, Shawn.

— *Rick McTague*

We would jointly like to thank Stefan Grünwedel at IDG Books for his professionalism and his talents throughout this project. We would also like to thank Howard Tayler for his technical contributions to this book.

We also thank KC Sue and Marcy Shanti at Novell Press, and Jim Sumser at IDG Books Worldwide, for making this book possible.

Contents at a Glance

Contents

Chapter 5   Personal Calendaring and Task Management   79

Chapter 6   Group Calendaring and Task Management   97

CHAPTER 1

Introduction to GroupWise 5.5

In this chapter, you learn about the GroupWise 5.5 *client interface*. The GroupWise *client* is the software you use to communicate with a main Group-Wise system. An *interface* is the end-user's view of a program. It's what you (the user) manipulate to control the program. This chapter briefly introduces you to the main parts of the GroupWise 5.5 for Windows client interface.

There are different versions of GroupWise for the different platforms the program can run on, such as Windows 95, Windows 16-bit for Windows 3.*x,* Macintosh, and UNIX. GroupWise even has a special WebAccess client that can be used through any of the popular Internet browsing programs, such as Microsoft Internet Explorer and Netscape Navigator. Each version has basically the same features, but the way you access those features can vary depending on the capabilities of the environment.

Nevertheless, all GroupWise 5 users deal with common message formats. Because the message format is consistent, each client version can recognize the format of a message and display it in the recipient's native environment, regardless of the client version used to create the message. Consequently, you can send messages to people who use different computing platforms without knowing how to use those platforms. For examples, you can use the Windows 95 version of GroupWise 5.5 to schedule meetings with people who use the WebAccess client or UNIX client.

Starting GroupWise

To launch GroupWise, simply double-click the GroupWise 5 shortcut icon on your desktop. Normally, GroupWise simply opens up your Mailbox.

The first time you run GroupWise, you may see the GroupWise Startup screen. You use this screen to configure your user ID, post office information, and TCP/IP settings. Don't panic if you encounter this screen—your system administrator can give you all the necessary information. We'll assume for the rest of the chapter that you don't need to deal with the Startup screen.

Appendix A provides more information about the Startup screen.

TIP

The Main GroupWise Screen

When you open the GroupWise 5 client, the screen in Figure 1.1 appears automatically. You access all GroupWise 5.5 features from the screen shown in Figure 1.1. We'll call this part of the interface the *main GroupWise screen*. From the main GroupWise screen, you access your incoming messages, outgoing messages, deleted messages, documents stored in a GroupWise library, and any items on your calendar. The GroupWise interface looks similar to other Windows 95 applications — in particular, it looks a lot like Windows 95 Explorer.

FIGURE 1.1 *The GroupWise 5.5 Interface*

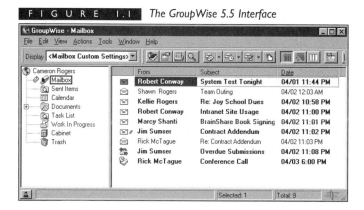

TIP

You can open multiple GroupWise windows and customize each one with a different view of your GroupWise information.

As you can see in Figure 1.1, there are five principle areas of the main screen:

- ▸ **Menu:** The GroupWise options menu under the title bar.
- ▸ **Toolbar:** Buttons that provide shortcuts to commonly used menu options.
- ▸ **Folders List:** The list of folder icons where your messages are stored.
- ▸ **Items Area:** The area where messages and other information in a selected folder appear.

▶ **Summary:** An indicator that shows the number of selected messages in the selected folder.

The Folders List and Items Area

The two most useful parts of the main GroupWise screen are the Folders List and the Items area. The Folders List contains a hierarchical structure of folders that are used to organize and hold messages and documents. The Items Area displays the individual messages that are located in the selected folder. The Folders List and items area are linked to each other. To view the items in a folder, select the folder in the Folders List on the left; the items in that folder will appear in the Items Area on the right.

There are eight folders that appear automatically in the main GroupWise screen. In Chapter 4, you learn how to adjust the settings for these folders and how to create new folders for storing your messages. Table 1.1 lists the eight system-generated default folders and describes their functions.

T A B L E 1.1	Default Folders
FOLDER NAME	**DESCRIPTION**
Mailbox	Contains the incoming messages you receive
Sent Items	Stores copies of the message you have sent
Calendar	Contains your calendar, which stores information about your appointments, notes, and tasks
Documents	Contains subfolders that display the documents you have authored and documents in your default library (document management is explained in Chapter 8)
Task List	Holds a list of your tasks
Work In Progress	Keeps drafts of unsent messages until you're ready to send them
Cabinet	Holds all of the messages that you file for storage (it's like your real-world filing cabinet)
Trash	Contains items you delete

The following subsections describe each of the default system folders in more detail.

Mailbox

When you want to see your new messages, you must open the Mailbox folder. When you receive a new message, an unopened envelope appears next to the Mailbox folder.

Open the Mailbox by single-clicking it. You will see a list of your opened and unopened messages in the Items Area to the right of the Mailbox, as shown in Figure 1.2. To read a message, simply double-click the message line. The text portion of the message will appear on the screen.

Sent Items

The Sent Items folder is your out box. This folder is used to manage messages you have sent. The Sent Items folder enables you to perform three handy tasks:

- ▶ Viewing the status of messages you have sent

- ▶ Resending messages

- ▶ Retracting messages you have sent (provided they have not been opened yet)

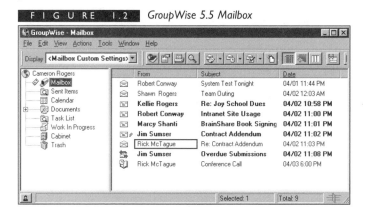

F I G U R E   1.2   *GroupWise 5.5 Mailbox*

Figure 1.3 shows the Sent Items folder. The first time you double-click an item in the Sent Items folder, a dialog box will appear asking you what you want the double-click action to perform. You have the choice of either having the message open or having the status information appear. This choice only appears the first time you double-click a sent item. Your choice in this dialog box will become your default action. (You can change your mind later in GroupWise options by clicking Tools → Options → Environment.)

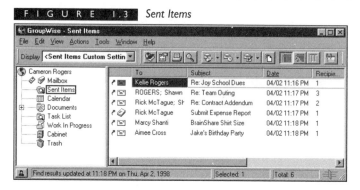

FIGURE 1.3   *Sent Items*

If you want to have the double-click action show you the status information, double-click a sent message. This shows you complete status information for the message, including when the message was delivered, opened, deleted, completed (if the message was a task), forwarded, accepted, or declined (if the message was an appointment or task).

The Sent Items folder is a special type of folder, known as a query folder. Folders are explained in more detail in Chapter 4.

From Sent Items, you can resend messages that have not been received for some reason. To resend a message, select the Resend option from the Send menu. When you edit and resend a message, you can retract the original message as long as it hasn't been opened yet.

To retract a message, highlight the message in the Sent Items screen and press the Delete key. Next, select Delete from All Mailboxes. This will delete the message from the recipient's Mailbox, as well as from your own Sent Items folder.

You can only retract e-mail messages that have not been opened.

IMPORTANT

Calendar

The Calendar is where you can create, view, and manage your Appointments, Tasks, and Notes. These Calendar items can be personal items (for example, a Personal Note to yourself), or they can be group items (for example, a Meeting Request). Figure 1.4 shows the Calendar.

FIGURE 1.4   *The Calendar*

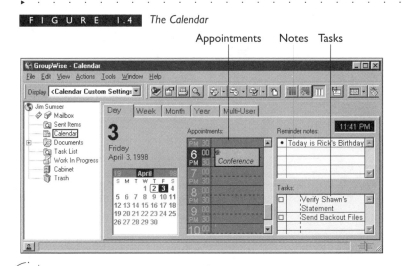

Appointments   Notes   Tasks

NOTE

Chapters 5 and 6 cover personal and group calendaring in more detail.

You can view your Calendar items in the Items area by clicking the Calendar folder. To view the Calendar as its own window, click Window and then choose Calendar. (If you have worked with previous versions of GroupWise, this is probably the Calendar view you are most familiar with.)

Task List

The Task List displays the tasks you have created for yourself, as well as those that have been sent to you. Figure 1.5 shows the Task List. (Tasks are explained in more detail in Chapters 5 and 6.)

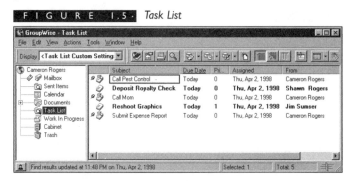

FIGURE 1.5 *Task List*

A task is something you need to complete. Each task has a start date and a due date. Overdue tasks are carried forward in the Calendar until you mark them complete.

If you send a task to someone else, and that person accepts it, you can track the task and find out when it is completed by looking in the Sent Items folder and viewing the task's status.

Work In Progress

You can use the Work In Progress folder to store drafts of messages that you haven't sent yet, as shown in Figure 1.6. If you begin writing a message and you realize you need some information that you don't have yet, save a draft of the message in this folder. When you get the missing information, you can add it to the saved message in the Work In Progress folder and then send the message along.

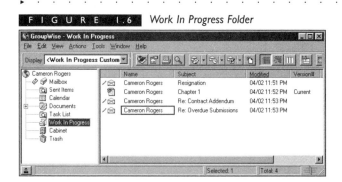

FIGURE 1.6 *Work In Progress Folder*

The Work In Progress folder is also useful for storing drafts of documents if you are using the document management features of GroupWise.

Cabinet

The Cabinet contains additional folders that you can use to organize your messages. See Figure 1.7 for an example of the Cabinet. Use the Cabinet folders to organize messages the same way you use the directory and subdirectory structure in Windows Explorer to organize files. You can place messages that pertain to the same project in a folder, nest folders inside other folders, and link messages to multiple folders. (Chapter 4 explains more about folders and how to manage your messages.)

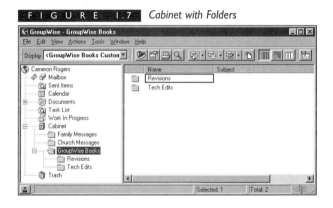

F I G U R E   1 . 7   *Cabinet with Folders*

Trash

When you delete a message from anywhere in GroupWise 5.5, the message goes into the Trash. Later, if you need to undelete the message, you can retrieve it from the Trash — provided that the Trash has not been emptied. (Chapter 4 discusses managing messages in the Trash folder.)

To view the messages in the Trash, simply click the Trash folder. Figure 1.8 shows how the Trash Folder looks when it's open. Messages do not remain in the Trash forever. They stay there for a certain period of time and then they are emptied from the Trash. When a message is emptied from the Trash, it is destroyed for good and there is no way to retrieve it. Messages are automatically emptied from the Trash after seven days. However, you can adjust the number of days that deleted messages stay in the Trash before they are automatically emptied. (Chapter 10 explains how to set this option.)

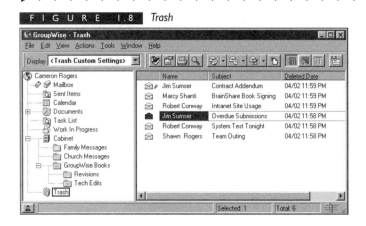

F I G U R E 1.8 *Trash*

Navigating Through GroupWise

There are many ways to perform individual tasks in GroupWise, and we will try to consistently show you the easiest steps to follow. Like other Windows applications, the GroupWise client contains pull-down menus; scroll bars; and minimize, maximize, and close buttons consistent with Windows 95 conventions. Figure 1.9 shows the GroupWise navigation controls.

F I G U R E 1.9 *GroupWise Navigation Controls*

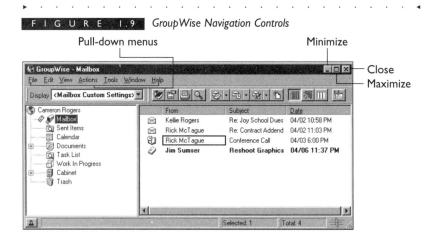

You can click any corner of the interface and drag it to a new position to change the size of the main GroupWise screen. You can also click and drag the dividing bar between different panes of the main screen to resize the panes. Likewise, you can click and drag messages from the Items Area to the Folders List.

Often, you can use alternative methods to execute the menu commands. For example, to send a Mail message, you can click the File menu, choose New, and Mail. Alternatively, you can simply click the Create New Mail button on the Toolbar.

There are several GroupWise features that can help you navigate through GroupWise more quickly. These features are the Toolbar, keystroke shortcuts, QuickMenus, and QuickViewer.

The Toolbar

The Toolbar, shown in Figure 1.10, is the row of buttons under the menu bar in the main GroupWise screen. You can use the buttons on the Toolbar as shortcuts to activate options under the pull-down menus. Using the Toolbar, you can quickly access the GroupWise features you use most often. Editing functions (such as Cut, Copy, and Paste), Spell Check, and Online Help are examples of buttons you can add to the Toolbar, saving you the trouble of selecting these options from the menus. You can use the Toolbar in message views as well as in the main GroupWise screen. (In Chapter 10, we explain how to customize your Toolbar.)

FIGURE 1.10 *Toolbar*

Toolbar

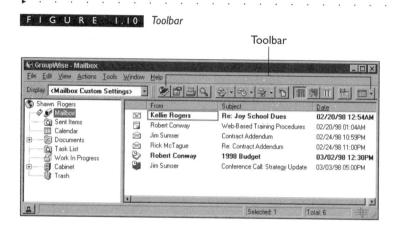

Keystroke Shortcuts

Most menu choices have corresponding keystroke combinations you can use to quickly select them. For example, you can refresh the current folder's message listing by choosing the Refresh option from the View menu, or you can press the F5 key and get the same result.

QuickMenus

QuickMenus, shown in Figure 1.11, are a feature of GroupWise 5 that add functionality to the right mouse button. When you are accessing different areas of the interface, a right-click of the mouse displays a short menu of actions.

QuickViewer

By enabling the GroupWise QuickViewer, you can read messages without double-clicking them. A third, lower window pane displays the contents of messages that have been selected, as shown in Figure 1.12. When you select a message in the Items Area, the QuickViewer pane of the main GroupWise screen displays the message contents automatically.

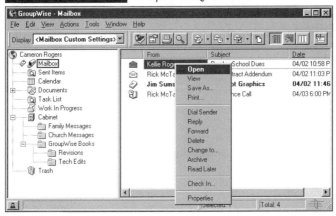

FIGURE 1.11 *GroupWise 5 QuickMenus*

FIGURE 1.12 *QuickViewer Enabled*

GroupWise Marquee

GroupWise Marquee is a ticker tape program that is installed to your desktop when you install GroupWise. The GroupWise Marquee runs constantly until you turn it off (see Figure 1.13). It constantly displays appointments and tasks that you need to complete in the near future. You can get details of the displayed item by placing the mouse pointer over the item in Marquee display.

TIP You can place the GroupWise Marquee in your Startup group to start whenever you turn on your computer.

FIGURE 1.13   *GroupWise Marquee*

GroupWise Desktop

The GroupWise Desktop is a mini GroupWise client. It conveniently displays a calendar letting you view your schedule and pending tasks at a glance. It can be resized to your liking by clicking and dragging the borders. You can perform many of the most common GroupWise tasks from the desktop, and you can launch the main GroupWise client from the desktop by clicking the toolbar buttons.

The GroupWise Desktop, as shown in Figure 1.14, is installed on your desktop when you install GroupWise. You can launch it anytime by simply double-clicking the icon, or you can place the icon in your Startup group for automatic startup when you turn on your computer.

FIGURE 1.14 *GroupWise Desktop*

Summary

In this chapter, you learned about the GroupWise 5 interface, which gives you access to many different messaging and calendaring functions. You also learned some tricks that will help you navigate through the interface. The next chapter covers the messaging features of GroupWise 5 in greater detail.

CHAPTER 2

Messaging Fundamentals

This chapter teaches you the fundamentals of GroupWise messaging. GroupWise is more than just an e-mail program: GroupWise is a personal time manager, a group scheduler, a document management system, a groupware program, and an e-mail program all rolled into one. As you saw in Chapter 1, there are several types of GroupWise messages. Typically, there are Mail messages, Phone messages, Appointments, Tasks, Reminder Notes, and workflow messages; other types of messages are available in enhanced GroupWise systems. You can send all of these message types to other users. You can also use GroupWise messages to keep track of your own schedule. Keep in mind that proper use of *all* message types is essential if you want to use GroupWise effectively.

GroupWise 5 uses icons to represent different message types and to reflect changes in the status of messages. By glancing at any icon in your Mailbox, you can identify which type of message it represents. You can also tell whether the message has file attachments, what its priority level is, and whether you have already opened the message.

Figure 2.1 shows how different message icons appear in the GroupWise mailbox when the corresponding messages are either opened or unopened. You should familiarize yourself with the different message icons so you can easily manage the different message types.

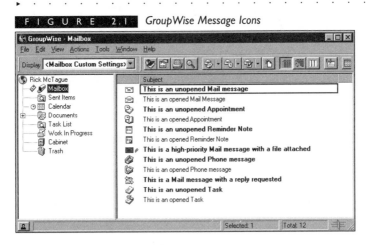

F I G U R E   2.1   *GroupWise Message Icons*

Other visual clues give different kinds of information about messages in the Mailbox. A paper clip next to a message indicates that the message includes a file attachment (or multiple attachments). A loudspeaker icon means that a sound file is attached. A red message icon indicates a high priority message, and a gray message icon indicates a low-priority message. (We explain how to set message priorities in Chapter 10.)

Message Types

When you're talking about GroupWise, the word "message" has many different meanings. You can send and receive five basic message types with GroupWise 5: Mail messages, Appointments, Tasks, Notes, Phone messages, and Discussions. (Additional message types are available if you have an enhanced system, such as Voice Mail messages and Fax messages. Check with your system administrator if you are not sure whether you system has enhanced capabilities.)

Mail Messages

A *Mail message* (also called an *e-mail message*) is like a memo. It has one or more recipients, a subject line, and a date. In addition, Mail messages contain fields where you can specify recipients of carbon copies and blind copies. We focus on Mail messages in this chapter.

To create a Mail message, click the Create New Mail icon on the Toolbar, or click File → New → Mail.

Appointments

You can create two types of Appointments: Meetings and Posted Appointments (known as "personal appointments" in previous versions of GroupWise). Posted Appointments are entries you make in your own Calendar to keep track of your personal engagements and to block out times in your Calendar when you are busy with important tasks. Meetings are group appointments that you can use to schedule meetings with other GroupWise users.

When another user sends you a request for a Meeting and you accept it, the Meeting automatically moves to your Calendar. If you decline a Meeting request, the message status information in the sender's Mailbox tells the sender that you have declined the meeting.

TIP Instead of using standard e-mail messages to schedule meetings, create GroupWise Meetings. Standard e-mail messages do not automatically create entries in recipients' Calendars. When you use standard e-mail messages for scheduling, recipients must take the time to mark their Calendars with Personal Appointments.

To create a Posted Appointment, click the down arrow button next to the Appointment icon on the Toolbar, and then click Posted Appointment.

NOTE Creating a Posted Appointment will not prevent others from scheduling you for meetings at that time, however, it will create a scheduling conflict if they do a busy search on your Calendar.

To create a Meeting, from the File menu click New and then Appointment. Alternatively, click the Create New Appointment button on the Toolbar.

Tasks

You can use a Task message to delegate or assign tasks to other GroupWise users. You can also create Personal Tasks for your personal Task List.

TIP Instead of using e-mail messages to delegate assignments, send a Task. Tasks automatically appear in the recipients' Task Lists, and you can conveniently specify a priority and a due date for each Task.

When someone receives and accepts a Task, the Task appears in the recipient's Task List folder and in the Task section of the recipient's Calendar view. The Task is carried forward each day until that person marks it as "Completed." If the recipient does not mark a Task completed by the specified due date, the Task turns red in both the Task List and in the Calendar view.

Reminder Notes

You can use Reminder Notes to create notes for yourself or to send reminders to other GroupWise users. When someone receives and accepts a Reminder Note, the Reminder Note automatically moves to the Notes: field in the recipient's Calendar view. Unlike a Task, however, a Reminder Note is not carried over from day to day. You enter Reminder Notes into the Calendar only on the date specified.

TIP If you want to create a Reminder Note that appears regularly — for example, to remind yourself when it's payday — you can use the Auto-Date feature, further explained in Chapter 6.

To create a Personal Reminder Note, open your Calendar view and double-click inside the Notes: field. To send someone else a Reminder Note, click File → New → Reminder Note.

Send Reminder Notes to members of your workgroup notifying them of days and times when you will be away from your desk, in meetings, or on vacation. This action will remind the people in your workgroup where you are on the specified days.

Phone Messages

Use Phone messages to inform other GroupWise users about phone calls you have taken for them. A Phone message is similar to an e-mail message. The Phone message window includes fields for caller information (such as name, company, and phone number) and a description of the call ("Urgent," "Please call," "Returned your call," and so forth). Phone messages are basically electronic versions of preprinted phone message forms.

To create a Phone message or While You Were Out message, click File → New → Phone message.

Because Phone messages are so similar to regular e-mail messages, with the exception of the fields in the view, we will not discuss them further.

Discussions

A Discussion is a special type of message that you use with Shared Folders. We will explain Discussions in Chapter 10.

Alternate E-mail Views

Views are display formats for GroupWise messages and interface components. For example, a mail message has two views associated with it: Mail and Simple Mail. You can choose a view that excludes the features you don't need or one that has a larger-than-normal message area.

 Alternate views do not prevent you from using all of the GroupWise features. In alternate views, you may not see certain shortcut methods for activating features, but you can always use the pull-down menus to access those features.

NOTE

The Simple Mail view provides a concise message area without the CC: or BC: buttons or the shortcut buttons to Send, Cancel, Address, or Attach files, as shown in Figure 2.2. Use this view when you need to send a short message to someone.

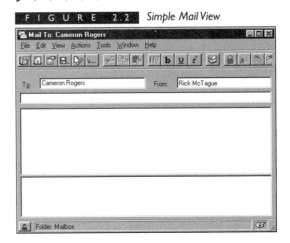

FIGURE 2.2 Simple Mail View

To send an e-mail message using the Simple Mail view, click the down arrow next to the Send Mail Message button on the Toolbar and select Mail (simple), or click the Change Item Type button on the Toolbar, highlight Simple Mail in the Views: list, and select OK.

You can also choose from different views with some other GroupWise message types, such as Phone messages.

Sending GroupWise Messages

The GroupWise dialog box for sending messages is very easy to use. The message dialog box is essentially a form you complete for each message you send. While the different message types may have different fields to fill in, several fields are common to all message types. In this section we focus on sending e-mail messages, but the concepts are basically the same for all GroupWise message types.

To send a message, you must enter someone's e-mail address. This might be an Internet e-mail message, such as bob@acme.com, or another GroupWise user's User ID, such as robertb. GroupWise also has a neat feature known as *automatic name completion*. If you begin typing someone's name in the To: line, GroupWise looks at the address book and tries to finish the name for you automatically. For example, if you were sending a message to Susan Alexander, you might type "Susan Al" and GroupWise would automatically finish the name for you. You can also use the Address Book to enter one or more user addresses. (Chapter 3 covers the Address Book in depth.)

The Send Mail view is shown in Figure 2.3.

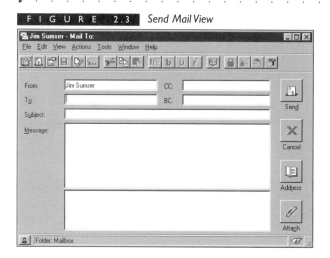

FIGURE 2.3 *Send Mail View*

To send an e-mail message:

1. Click File → New → Mail. Alternatively, you can click the Mail button on the Toolbar.

TIP   Because the Toolbar buttons are not labeled, you can identify the action of each button by simply placing the mouse pointer over the button. After a slight delay, a pop-up help box will appear describing the button's function.

2. Select the recipients using the Address Book or by typing their names in the To:, CC:, and BC: fields. Separate multiple user names with commas.

3. Add a subject line in the Subject: field.

4. Type your message in the Message: field.

5. Click the Send button to send the message.

The recipients listed in the To: field are the primary recipients of the message. Primary recipients can view the message information screen and see all the other primary recipients and all CC: (carbon copy) recipients, but they cannot see the names of the BC: (blind copy) recipients. The people listed in the CC: field receive a copy of the message. Carbon copy recipients can also see all of the primary recipients, but they cannot see blind copy recipients. People who receive a blind copy can see all primary recipients and all carbon copy recipients, but they cannot see other blind copy recipients.

If you want to send a message to multiple people, but you don't want any of them to know who else received the message, make them all blind copy recipients. For example, you could use this technique to inform job applicants that a position has been filled if you don't want the applicants to know who else applied for the job. Because a name in the To: field is required, you can insert your own name.

Saving Draft Messages in the Work In Progress Folder

As you compose a message, you might find a need to save your work and resume your message later. You can save messages you are working on in the Work In Progress folder.

To save a message in the Work In Progress folder:

1. With the message open, choose Save Draft from the File menu.

2. Select the Work In Progress folder and click OK.

WiseGuide: Here's an alternative way to save a message in the Work In Progress folder: When you decide you need to work on a message later, click the Cancel button. You are prompted to save the message. Choose Yes, and save the message in the Work In Progress folder.

To resume working on a draft message:

1. Open the Work In Progress folder.

2. Double-click the message you want to finish.

3. Finish the message and choose Send.

A message can be saved as a draft message at any point during its composition. You can also attach files to a message; they will be saved along with the message in the Work In Progress folder.

If you modify a file that is attached to a message in the Work In Progress folder, be sure you delete the file attachment icon and reattach the message. Otherwise, the original version of the file will be sent.

Attaching Files to a Message

You can share documents, spreadsheets, database files, or other files by sending them to other users as file attachments to a GroupWise message. You can attach files to any GroupWise message, even if the message type does not include a file attachment field in the dialog box.

To attach a file to an e-mail message:

1. In the e-mail dialog box, click the Attach button.

2. Select the file to attach.

3. Click OK. The file attachment appears in the file attachment window, as shown in Figure 2.4.

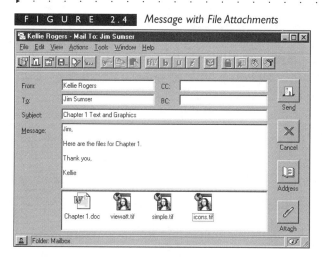

F I G U R E   2 . 4   *Message with File Attachments*

You can also attach document references and object linking and embedding (OLE) objects, such as charts or spreadsheets, to GroupWise messages. We'll explain how document references work in Chapter 8. To attach an OLE object to a GroupWise message:

1. From the e-mail message view, click File → Attachments → Attach Object.

2. Choose Create New to create a new object using the associated application. The Insert Object dialog box appears as shown in Figure 2.5.

3. Select the type of object you want to create.

4. Click OK to open the *server application*, or the application you will use to create the object.

5. Create the object you want to embed.

6. In the server application, click File → Exit.

7. Select Yes to update the object into your message view.

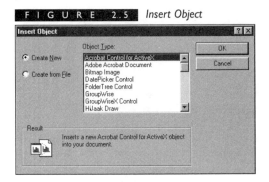

F I G U R E   2 . 5   *Insert Object*

After you attach a file, object, or document reference, an icon representing the attachment appears at the bottom of the e-mail window. The attached file or object will travel along with your message to the recipient.

Reading Messages

The messages you receive are initially stored in your Mailbox folder (also called simply "the Mailbox"). To read a message:

1. Click the Mailbox to display a list of the messages you have received in the Items Area.

2. Double-click the desired message, or highlight the message and press Enter.

The message opens for you to read.

TIP

Use the QuickViewer to quickly read several messages in succession. To activate the QuickViewer, click View → QuickViewer. A third pane will open at the bottom of the GroupWise window and will display the contents of the message you have highlighted.

Viewing File Attachments

When you receive a message with a file attachment, you can use the built-in viewers in GroupWise to view the file's contents. From a viewer screen, you can launch the associated application or save the attachment. Figure 2.6 shows a file attachment opened by a viewer.

F I G U R E   2 . 6   *File Attachment Opened by a Viewer*

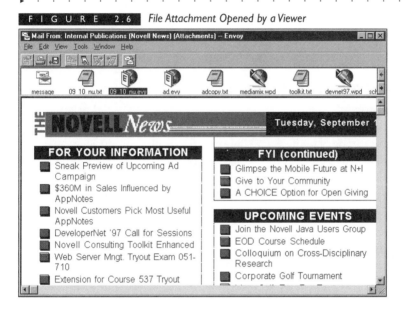

The first time you view a file attachment, GroupWise generates the viewers for all supported file formats. GroupWise only generates the viewers the first time you view an attachment after GroupWise is installed (or if you have installed updated viewer files), and it usually takes less than a minute to generate them.

The first time you receive a Mail message with an attachment and double-click the attachment icon, you will be prompted to indicate what function you want double-clicking to launch. You can choose to have attachments open in their default application (choose Yes to the Environment option) or in the GroupWise viewer (choose No to the environment option. If you change your mind later, you can adjust this setting using the Options feature under the Tools menu).

To view a file attachment from an open message, double-click the attachment icon (if you selected View as the default action), or right-click the attachment icon and select View Attachment.

To launch an application associated with the attached file, double-click the attachment icon (if you selected Open as the default action), or right-click the attachment icon and select Open.

NOTE

The first time you view an attachment, GroupWise generates the required viewer files, which causes a slight delay. This only happens the first time you view a file after the GroupWise software has been installed or updated.

Replying to Messages

GroupWise enables you to have electronic conversations and maintain a record of what each person says. When you respond to another person's message, you can reply to the sender only or reply to all recipients of the message. You can also include the original message in your reply. When you include a copy of the original message, you can insert your comments at the top of the message or at various points throughout the message. Figure 2.7 shows your message reply options.

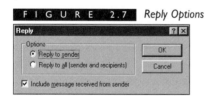

F I G U R E   2.7 *Reply Options*

To reply to a message:

1. While the message is open, click Reply.

2. Choose either Reply to Sender or Reply to All.

3. By default, the "Include message received from sender" option is selected. Deselect this option if you do not want to include a copy of the original message in your response.

Use the Reply to All option judiciously. Make sure that everyone who received the original message really needs to see your reply.

The sender's name (and all recipients' names if you selected Reply to All) automatically appears in the To: field. The Subject: field of the original message is retained, with the abbreviation "Re:" in front of it. If you left the Include Message Received from Sender option selected, the original message text appears in the reply message. When you type your reply, it appears above the original message unless you move the cursor to another location.

Reply messages do not automatically include the file attachments from the original message. You can, however, attach files to a reply message.

Forwarding Messages

If you want to pass along a message or its file attachment to someone else, you should forward the message. When you forward a message, you send a new message with the old message as an attachment. The original message remains intact along with its file attachments, as shown in Figure 2.8. It is a good idea to always include your own introductory message when you forward a message.

To forward a message, do the following:

1. While the message to be forwarded is open, click the Forward button or choose Forward from the Actions menu. A new message screen opens. The original message appears as an attachment with the message subject as the name of the attachment.

2. Use the Address Book (or enter the user names) to fill in the To: field and type a message to the recipient(s).

3. Click Send to forward the message.

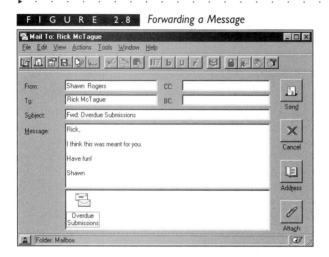

F I G U R E   2 . 8   *Forwarding a Message*

When you forward a message, you actually create a new message, which contains a copy of the original message and its file attachments. A copy of the original message remains in your Mailbox. You can delete the original message if you don't need it, or store it in a folder.

When a recipient opens the forwarded message, he or she accesses the original message and its file attachments by double-clicking the Mail message icon in the Attach: field.

Deleting Messages

When you no longer need a message, you can delete it from your Mailbox. After you delete it, the message goes to the Trash folder. The message remains there until you empty the Trash manually or until the Trash is emptied automatically, according to what you set up in GroupWise Options.

To delete a message, select the message and press the Delete key. Or, click the message and drag it to the Trash folder.

You can delete messages from any location (for example, from the Mailbox folder, the Sent Items folder, or from any Calendar view).

Restoring Messages

When you delete a message, it goes to the Trash folder and stays there until you empty the Trash — or until your Trash is automatically emptied according to the default options that are set for your GroupWise account. While the message is stored in the Trash, you can undelete or restore the message to its original location.

To restore a message to the location it was deleted from:

1. Open the Trash folder.

2. Highlight the message.

3. Choose Undelete from the Edit menu.

Alternatively, you can right-click the message and choose Undelete from the QuickMenu. The message will be restored to its previous location.

Purging Messages

To permanently delete a message, you can open the Trash folder and delete the message. You can also empty all messages from your Trash by right-clicking your Trash folder and selecting Empty.

Once messages have been emptied or deleted from Trash, they are no longer recoverable.

Summary

In this chapter, you learned the fundamentals of GroupWise messaging. We explained how to send and read messages, how to send replies, how to forward messages, and how to delete messages you no longer need. Chapter 3 explains how to use the GroupWise Address Book to further improve your productivity with GroupWise.

CHAPTER 3

Using the GroupWise Address Book

The GroupWise Address Book is your GroupWise yellow pages; it's your master directory for looking up information about other users. Just as a telephone book lists more than just telephone numbers, the Address Book lists more than just GroupWise user IDs. You can find other users' phone numbers, fax numbers, departments, and much more.

Use the Address Book to do the following:

▶ Find GroupWise user IDs when addressing GroupWise messages.

▶ Send messages to groups of users; for example, to all members of a specific department.

▶ Create personal groups that list the users you often send messages to.

▶ Look up information about other GroupWise users.

▶ Create personal address books that contain addresses of users within and outside of the GroupWise system, such as people you commonly correspond with on the Internet.

▶ Create address profiles, such as all users who have the job title, Director, or all users who work in a specific building.

▶ Dial your telephone (if GroupWise Conversation Place is enabled).

GroupWise Conversation Place is a telephone integration program that links GroupWise with your telephone system. If you don't know whether you can use Conversation Place, ask your system administrator.

Address Book Features

The main components of the Address Book are:

▶ Search fields

▶ Menus

▶ System and personal address books

▶ To:, BC:, and CC: fields

▶ Information field headings

Figure 3.1 shows the GroupWise Address Book with its main components labeled.

GroupWise Address Book

System Address Book   Personal Address Book   Search Fields

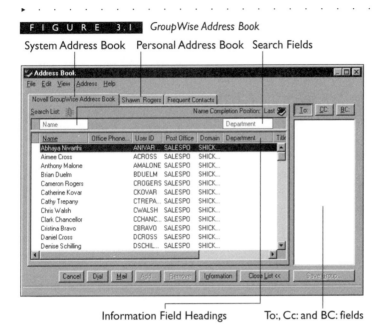

Information Field Headings   To:, Cc: and BC: fields

NOTE

When we refer to the *Address Book* (capitalized) we mean the Address Book program that is part of GroupWise. When we refer to *address book* (lowercase) we are referring to one of the individual directories — such as the system address book or the Frequent Contacts address book — that contain lists of users.

You can access the Address Book in a number of ways. For instance, you can run the Address Book as a standalone program outside of GroupWise. Used in this way, the Address Book is a handy company directory. If you create an Address Book icon in Windows 95, you can quickly access the Address Book to look up phone numbers, addresses, and other information.

To set up an icon for the Address Book in Windows 95:

I. Use Explorer or the My Computer icon to locate ADDRBOOK.EXE. (It is typically located in the NOVELL\GROUPWISE directory.)

2. Right-click the ADDRBOOK.EXE file and drag it to your desired location.

3. Choose the Create Shortcut Here option from the pop-up menu.

You can also use the Address Book to address GroupWise messages to people. To launch the Address Book from within GroupWise, choose Address Book from the Tools menu (or click the Address Book icon on the Toolbar).

Notice in Figure 3.1 that the Address Book has three tabs—one labeled Novell GroupWise Address Book, one labeled Frequent Contacts, and one with a GroupWise user name.

The Novell GroupWise address book (the system address book) is the master address book for your GroupWise system. All users in the system are visible in this address book.

The Frequent Contacts address book lists the users that you have recently sent messages to or received messages from. These users are listed in alphabetical order. The Frequent Contacts address book enables you to send messages quickly to the people you correspond with most often.

The address book tab with your name on it is a personal address book that you use to add names, e-mail addresses, and other personal information about users you correspond with. The users listed in the personal address book do not have to be GroupWise users (or even e-mail users, for that matter). You can use a personal address book to store all of your contact information. Later in this chapter, we'll explain how to create additional personal address books.

To switch between the various address books, simply click the appropriate tab.

To close an address book that you don't want to use, click the address book tab, and then choose Close Book from the File menu.

You can change the way information is displayed in the Address Book by moving or modifying the headings. To move a heading from one location to another, simply click and drag the heading to a new location. To remove a heading, click and drag it from the headings bar. To replace a heading that has been deleted, right-click the headings bar and select the heading you want to add. You can resize headings by clicking and dragging the line that separates two headings.

▶ · ◀

Addressing Messages with the Address Book

When sending a message to more than one person, it is usually easier to address GroupWise messages with the Address Book than it is to type in user names. Also, you don't need to worry about misspelling user names when you use the Address Book.

Use the arrow keys or the scroll bar to locate an addressee, and then double-click the user's name to insert that name in the To: field of the Address Book. Insert any additional names, and then choose OK to return to your message. The recipients will be inserted in the To: field of the message.

The user list is searchable. To find an addressee, begin typing the person's name. The address list quickly highlights the name that most closely matches what you type. (We'll talk more about different searching techniques later in this chapter.)

The right column (where the users are listed when you select them from the Address Book) defaults to the To: field. GroupWise assumes that most of the users you send the message to are the primary recipients and should be added to the message's To: field. Consequently, when you select users from the address list, they are listed in the To: field by default. To add BC: or CC: recipients, click the corresponding button before adding users.

If you have a user in the To: field that needs to be moved to either the CC: or BC: field, you can right-click the user name and choose the appropriate field from the QuickMenu. Alternatively, you can hold the Control button down, select multiple names that need to be moved to either CC: or BC:, and then click the CC: or BC: button.

Sending Messages to Groups

A GroupWise group is a list of users to which you can send messages. There are two types of address book groups: public groups and personal groups.

A public group is a list of users defined by the system administrator for convenient message addressing. All GroupWise users have access to the system's public groups, unless they have been excluded by the system administrator. For example, your system administrator may create a distribution list called Sales that includes all members of the sales organization. Public groups are located in the system address book.

A personal group is a list of users you create to automate your messaging. For example, you can create personal groups that include the members of each project you work on. (Personal groups only display in personal address books. They do not display in the system address book.)

Groups are listed in the Address Book along with individual users. They are distinguished from users by a group icon, as shown in Figure 3.2.

FIGURE 3.2 *Groups in the Address Book*

Groups

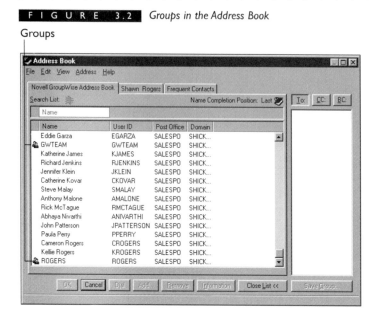

Addressing Messages to Groups

To address a message to a group:

1. Click the Address icon from within a message view.

2. Double-click the group to add the group name to the To: field, or select the group and click the To:, CC:, or BC: button to add the group name to the appropriate address field.

3. Click OK.

(If you know the name of the group, you don't have to use the Address Book. Just type the group name in your message's To: field.)

To search for groups, simply begin typing the name of the group. When GroupWise finds the group you want, you can stop typing.

If you want to send a message to most, but not all, members of a group, right-click the group and choose the Edit Group option. The members of the group will be listed individually in the To: field. You can then delete individual group members from the To: field.

Creating Personal Groups

You can create personal groups that appear in your personal address book. To create a personal group:

1. Open an address book (for example, the system address book) that contains the users you want to include in a personal group.

2. Add the users you want in the group to the To:, CC:, and BC: fields in the same manner you would use when addressing a message.

3. Click the Save Group button.

4. Name the group, specify which personal address book the group should be added to, and then click OK.

You can include users from different address books in one group.

Creating Personal Address Books

Personal address books are address books you create that list users you often correspond with. Personal address books can contain users who are in the GroupWise system or users who are external to the GroupWise system, such as Internet users. (Remember, the Novell GroupWise address book is the system address book and only the administrator can add to or modify the listings in this address book.)

NOTE Personal groups are customized groupings of users that you can address messages to by typing the group name in the To: field. Personal address books are like personal Rolodexes. In personal address books, you can store information about users, organizations, or resources.

You can create an unlimited number of personal address books within the Address Book to organize your contacts. For example, you can create separate personal address books for key contacts in other companies, for your friends and family, and for people you correspond with over the Internet.

By default, GroupWise creates one personal address book for you. Your personal address book has your name on the address book tab.

To create a new personal address book, do the following:

1. With the Address Book open, click File → New Book.

2. Name the new address book and choose OK. The address book tab will appear in the main Address Book window.

3. Click the Add button.

4. Choose Person, Resource, or Organization.

5. Fill in the fields for the entry.

6. Click OK.

Keep in mind the following points about personal address books:

▸ You can create, edit, and save any number of personal address books.

▸ You can add and delete names and address information for any person, resource, or company in your personal address books, but you cannot modify information in your system address book.

▸ The same name can be included in multiple address books. If you copy an entry from one address book to another and then later modify the entry, it will be updated in all address books that contain the entry.

▸ Internet addresses can be included in personal address books.

▸ You do not have to display all address books in the Address Book main window. To choose which books you want open, use the Open Book and Close Book options in the File menu to specify which address books appear.

▸ You can define custom fields for your personal address books. See the topic, "Create My Own Fields and Columns" in the Address Book online help system for instructions.

TIP **To send a message to everyone in a personal address book, click the address book tab to make the address book active, choose Edit, Select All, and then click the To: button.**

To edit an entry in a personal address book, highlight the entry, and choose Edit from the Edit menu.

To delete a personal address book:

1. Click File.

2. Click Delete Book.

3. Highlight the book or books you want to delete.

4. Click OK.

5. Click Yes to confirm the deletion.

Searching the Address Book

You can search for Address Book information by using the Search List box, by using a predefined address filter, or by defining your own filter.

Search List Box

To search for an address using the Search List box:

1. Click the tab of the address book you want to search.

2. In the Search List box, begin typing what you are searching for. GroupWise will place information that matches your search criteria in the search box.

3. When GroupWise finds the information you are searching for, click the To: field to insert the address.

Figure 3.3 shows the Search List box.

FIGURE 3.3 *Address Book Search Fields*

Search Fields

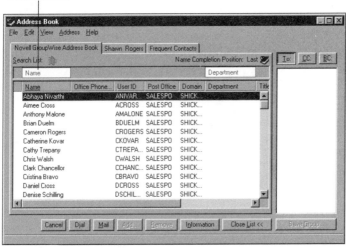

Predefined Address Filters

In GroupWise, a filter refers to a set of conditions that remove selected items from a list. For example, you can use a message filter to stop unopened messages from appearing in your Mailbox or an address book filter to display only resources or groups. You'll learn more about using filters in Chapter 4.

By default, address books display all entries that have been incorporated into them. Consequently, in large address books, individuals and groups can be difficult to locate. By using a predefined filter, you can display only the information you are looking for.

The Address Book has four predefined filters: Filter for Groups, Filter for People, Filter for Organizations, and Filter for Resources. In addition, you can define your own customized address filters.

To use a predefined filter while using the Address Book:

1. Click View.

2. Click Predefined Filters.

3. Click the filter you want to use.

After you enable filtering, a check mark appears next to the Filtering Enabled option on the View menu and a filter icon appears at the upper left of an address book tab. Only the users, groups, organizations, or resources specified in the filter appear in the address list.

Figure 3.4 shows the GroupWise Address Book filtered to show only resources. Notice that the filter icon appears next to the Search List field.

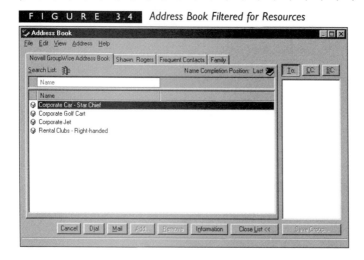

F I G U R E   3 . 4   *Address Book Filtered for Resources*

To return to the regular (nonfiltered) Address Book view, click View and then click the Filtering Enabled checkbox to remove the check mark and disable filtering.

User-defined Filters

You can design customized filters to help you with common address book searches. For example, if you often send a message to all managers in a company, you might define a filter that searches for all managers. By using this filter to send a message to managers, you ensure that the message is sent to people with that title.

Using customized filters is often more efficient than creating personal groups because groups quickly become outdated. A filter ensures that only current users in the address book receive your message.

To create a filter:

1. Click View.

2. Click Define Filter. The Filter dialog box appears. The first column lists the columns available in the address book.

3. Click a column.

4. Click the Operator drop-down box to select an operator.

5. Type a parameter in the Parameter text box. By default, the Parameter drop-down box displays End.

6. If you want to choose additional parameters, click the Parameter drop-down box and choose an operator.

7. Repeat Steps 3–6 to establish additional filter criteria.

8. When you have defined the filter, choose End in the final parameter's drop-down box, and then click OK.

An operator is a symbol that represents a mathematical operation. A parameter is a variable used with a command to indicate a specific value or option. For example, to create a filter that lists only users with the last name Williams, click the Last Name column, click the = button (the equal sign button), and then type Williams. In this example, = is the operator and Williams is the parameter.

Here is another example. Suppose you want to create a filter that addresses a message to all managers in the sales department of your company. Follow these steps:

1. Click View.

2. Select Define Filter.

3. Click the Column drop-down list and select Department.

4. Click the Operator box and choose =.

5. Enter the name of the department (for example, Sales) in the Parameter box.

6. Click the Parameter drop-down box and choose And.

7. Click the Column drop-down list and select Title.

8. Click the Operator box and choose =.

9. Enter Manager in the Parameter box.

10. Choose End from the Parameter drop-down list.

11. Choose OK to apply the filter.

Figure 3.5 shows the filter dialog box for the previous example.

F I G U R E   3.5 *Sales Manager Filter*

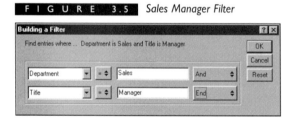

Sharing Personal Address Books

You can easily share an address book you create with other GroupWise users, who can then use the address book you create.

Suppose you maintain an address book for a specific department. You can share the department address book with other users by following these steps:

1. Create the custom address book and populate it with the user information.

2. Click File → Sharing. The sharing dialog box appears as shown in Figure 3.6.

3. Click the Shared With option.

4. Enter the names or groups with whom this address book should be shared in the Name: field.

5. Specify the access rights the user should have. In most cases, the recipients of your shared address book only need read access.

6. Click OK. A dialog box will appear enabling you to customize the message that the recipient of the shared address book will receive.

7. Click OK to share the address book. The recipients will receive a message indicating that you have shared an address book with them. They will have the opportunity to accept or decline the shared address book.

FIGURE 3.6 *Sharing an Address Book*

You can use the Address Book's export and import features to share personal address books with other users.

To export an address book:

1. Open the address book you wish to export.

2. Click File → Export.

3. Choose Entire Address Book or Selected Items.

4. Name the address book file. (Address book export files have a .NAB file extension.)

5. Choose Save.

You can now send this file to other users as an attachment to a message. They can then import the file.

To import a personal address book file:

1. Highlight the personal address book to which the group will be imported, or create a new personal address book to contain the imported users.

2. Click File → Import.

3. Locate the .NAB file and choose Open.

You cannot import users into your system address book.

Using the Address Book to Call Other Users

If GroupWise Conversation Place has been enabled on your system, you can use the Address Book to dial other users on the telephone automatically. To dial a phone number from the Address Book:

1. Locate the person you wish to dial in an address book.

2. Click Dial. If an address entry contains only one phone number, the Address Book dials that number. If there is more than one number, you are prompted for which number you want to use.

3. If prompted for the phone number, choose a phone number from the Available Numbers dialog box and click OK.

Integration with Other Address Books

GroupWise supports integration with other vendors' address books. For example, if your system supports another e-mail program, you might be able to use that e-mail program's address book along with the GroupWise Address Book.

To integrate another vendor's address book in GroupWise:

1. Open Control Panel.

2. Double-click the Mail icon.

3. Select Add.

4. Follow the prompts to add the vendor's address service.

You should contact your system administrator to determine if you can use another vendor's address book with your GroupWise program.

TIP

The dialog box you see after Step 2, of the previous list, is also the dialog box you use to determine the order in which address books are searched by the GroupWise name completion feature.

Summary

In this chapter we explained how to use the GroupWise Address Book to automate mail message addressing and to organize information about people you frequently correspond with. In Chapter 4, we explain how to manage your messages efficiently to prevent information overload.

CHAPTER 4

Message Management

As messaging technology advances, more and more message types are being created. In a standard GroupWise system, the Mailbox displays Mail messages, Phone messages, Appointments, Tasks, Notes, and Documents.

With GroupWise add-on products, the Mailbox can also display other kinds of messages, such as Fax messages and Voice Mail messages. With all of these different message types available, you need some way to manage your messages, to prevent information overload and to eliminate clutter from your GroupWise Mailbox. This chapter explains how to use different GroupWise features to organize and manage your messages.

Finding Messages

The main tool used to look for messages and documents throughout your mailbox and any document management library that you have rights to is Find. Using Find to look for documents is covered in Chapter 8.

Find is a simple yet powerful utility that returns a "results" window (for your database — heads out there, a "query"). The results can then be read, deleted, moved to a folder, saved, printed, or archived — everything we're going to talk about in this chapter!

To start a Find session, simply click the Find option in the Tools menu.

You can create very simple requests to find items. For example, the query shown in Figure 4-1, looks for messages that have the word "meet" in the subject line or anywhere in the contents of a message (that is, a "full text" search).

FIGURE 4.1 *Simple Find Dialog Box*

Notice that the mailbox (and any folder underneath) can be selected in the Look in: area of this screen, as well as libraries.

Once the Find criteria has been specified in this box, click OK to execute the search. The GroupWise Find Results screen displays (see Figure 4-2), listing the messages and items that are found.

FIGURE 4.2 *Find Results Screen*

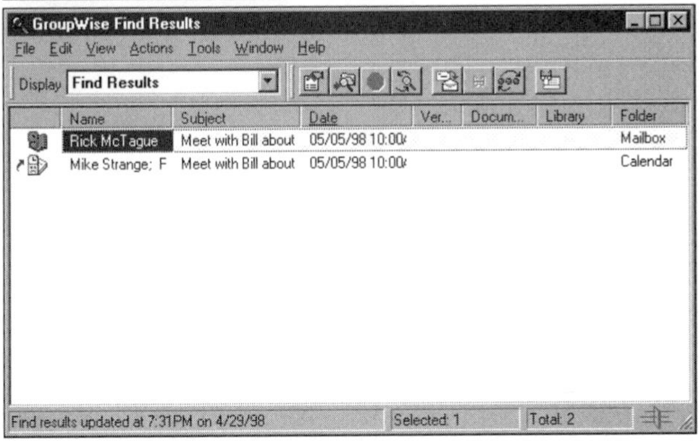

Once the results have been displayed, you can act on the messages just like you would normally, or perform any other action.

TIP As you will see later in this chapter, you can save the results of a find as a "Find Results Folder," which performs the search every time you access the contents of the folder.

A more in-depth search can be created using filters, which are discussed in depth later in this chapter. Figure 4.3 shows a find session that looks for all high-priority appointments from Chris.

To add more criteria to the Find session, select other items such as message type, who the message was from, the disposition of the message (sent, received, and so on), and a date range for the age of the message. To add advanced search criteria beyond what is available in this dialog box (such as message priority of high), click the Advanced Find button and you can craft a search that will boggle the mind.

The Advanced Find dialog box (see Figure 4-4) is exactly like the Filter dialog box, which we cover later in this chapter.

F I G U R E   4.3 *Find Dialog Screen with More Criteria*

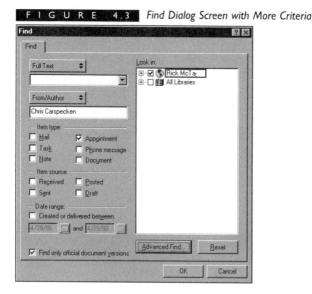

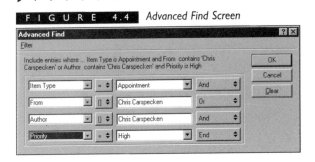

F I G U R E   4 . 4 *Advanced Find Screen*

Archiving Messages

The primary method for storing messages indefinitely is called archiving. An archived message is not stored in your Mailbox (which is on a GroupWise server), rather it is stored on your local hard drive or in your user directory on the network. Archiving messages gives you access to your old messages without cluttering up your active Mailbox. You can archive messages that have been sent to you as well as messages you have sent to others. The process of archiving messages is fairly easy. In fact, you can set up the GroupWise 5 client so archiving happens automatically when messages have been sitting in your Mailbox for a certain period of time.

NOTE

You cannot archive messages when using GroupWise Remote or GroupWise WebAcess.

Before you can archive messages, you must specify a location where your archived messages will be stored. This location is usually on your hard drive. If you have questions about the location of your archive directory, ask your system administrator.

To specify an archive directory:

I. Click Tools → Options.

2. Double-click the Environment icon and choose the File Location tab, as shown in Figure 4.5.

3. Enter a directory path in the Archive directory field, or browse to a directory on your hard drive.

4. Click OK and then Close.

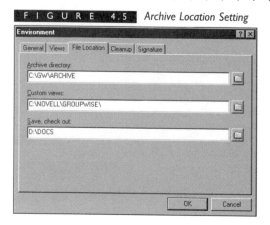

FIGURE 4.5 *Archive Location Setting*

To archive messages:

1. From a folder (for example, the Mailbox or the Sent Items folder), select a message or group of messages. (You can select a range of messages by pressing Shift and clicking the beginning and end of the range. You can select multiple, nonadjacent messages by pressing Ctrl and clicking the messages.)

2. Choose Actions.

3. Choose Archive.

The selected messages move to your local archive storage file.

NOTE Optionally, you can right mouse click the message or group of messages you want to archive and choose Archive from the QuickMenu.

To have GroupWise automatically archive messages after a certain length of time, click Tools → Options → Environment → Cleanup. (See Chapter 10 for customizing these options.) You can adjust the period of time that Mail messages, Phone messages, Appointments, Tasks, and Notes remain in your Mailbox before they are automatically archived. Automatic archiving will then take place as needed each time you exit GroupWise.

Viewing Archived Messages

To view an archived message:

1. Select File, and then choose Open Archive. The messages stored in the Archive Mailbox are listed. As Figure 4.6 illustrates, (Archive) appears

on the title bar to indicate that you are looking at archived messages. If you view the File menu again, you see that a check mark appears next to the Open Archive option. The check mark indicates that the archive is currently open.

2. Double-click the message you want to read. If you are using the QuickViewer (see Chapter 1), the contents of the archived message appear in the bottom message pane.

To return to your Mailbox from an archive, click File and then deselect Open Archive. The active folder and its contents appear. If you look at the File menu again, you see there is no longer a check mark next to the Open Archive option. The check mark disappears when the regular Mailbox is active, and (Archive) disappears from the title bar.

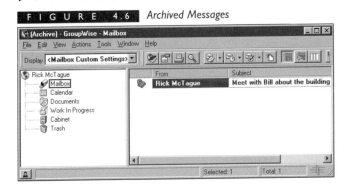

FIGURE 4.6 *Archived Messages*

Unarchiving Messages

To unarchive a message or group of messages, do the following:

1. With your Archive Mailbox open, select the message or group of messages you want to move back to your active Mailbox.

2. Click Actions and then deselect Archive. (The Archive option is a toggle switch. When a message is archived, a check mark appears next to the Archive option in the File menu.)

The selected messages will be removed from your hard drive on a GroupWise server. You should now be able to see the messages in their original folder.

Saving Messages

Saving messages is different from archiving. When you save a message, you transfer the message information into a separate file. This file can then be used in a word processing program or other application. When you archive a message, the message is not deleted from your Mailbox; GroupWise merely saves a copy of it in a separate file.

To save a message:

1. From the Mailbox folder, select the message and then choose Save As under the File menu.

2. As Figure 4.7 shows, highlight the message, specify the destination directory and filename for the message, and click Save to save the message as a file. The message is saved as a WordPerfect-compatible document. A default filename is created from the Subject: field (you can create your own filename) and the extension .MLM is added to the end of the filename.

NOTE   When you save a message as an individual file, it does not maintain the properties on the item (such as priority or security), and the formatting is similar to what you get when you print the message.

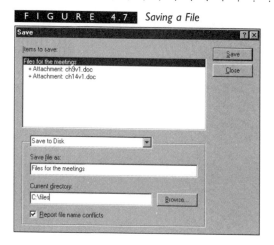

FIGURE 4.7   *Saving a File*

Printing Messages

The Print option under the File menu enables you to specify custom print settings. To select paper type, fonts, and other options:

1. Click the File menu.
2. Choose Print.
3. Choose Properties.
4. The dialog box shown in Figure 4.8 appears. Select the desired tab, set the options you want, and click OK.

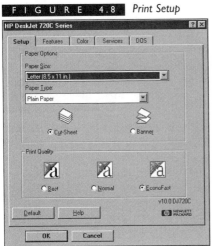

FIGURE 4.8 *Print Setup*

This dialog box is unique for each type of printer you have installed.

NOTE

To print messages:

1. Select the messages you want to print.
2. Choose Print from the File menu (or press Ctrl+P).
3. Select either the message or the attachment you would like to print.
4. Click the Print button.

NOTE The "Print attachment with associated application" option launches the application associated with the file attachment and prints the attachment from that application (for example, from WordPerfect). Use this option if you want to preserve the formatting of the file attachment.

Organizing Messages with the Cabinet

You use the Cabinet to organize and store your message folders. You can organize folders in the Cabinet the same way you organize directories in Windows 3.1, or folders in Windows 95 and on the Mac OS.

The folders in your Cabinet fall into three categories—personal folders, shared folders, and find results folders.

You create personal folders for your own, private use. Use them to organize your messages and documents into separate groups. For example, you can create folders for information pertaining to certain projects, for specific message types, or for messages from certain individuals.

You can also create shared folders. Shared folders contain messages that can be viewed by other users. The creator of a shared folder determines the access rights to the folder. For example, when you create a shared folder, you can decide who will be able to read the messages in the folder, who can add messages to that folder, and so forth.

Find results folders are used to display a fresh listing of items that are the results of a Find session. For example, a High Priority Items folder can do a fresh search of your entire mailbox for messages that have a priority of High. Each time you click this folder, the search is performed again, so the listing is updated. The Find tool was covered earlier in this chapter.

NOTE The Sent Items and Task List folders are Find Results folders.

Creating Folders

GroupWise folders work the same way as the subdirectory structure of your computer's hard drive. When you open GroupWise 5, your folders appear on the left side of the screen. Your name should automatically appear on the top-level folder (the user folder). In addition to your user folder, there are eight default GroupWise folders—Mailbox, Sent Items, Calendar, Documents, Task List, Work In Progress, Cabinet, and Trash.

You can only add new folders in the Cabinet, in your user folder, in the Documents folder and in the Work In Progress folder. We recommend that you store most of your GroupWise messages in Cabinet folders. You can organize the folders and subfolders in your Cabinet any way you like.

In GroupWise, folder names can include punctuation and spaces.

TIP

Figure 4.9 shows some typical folders. A button with a plus sign to the left of a folder indicates that the folder contains hidden subfolders. A button with a minus sign to the left of a folder means that the folder has been expanded to show all of its subfolders. Click a plus or minus button to show or hide the substructure beneath a particular folder.

F I G U R E   4.9 *Cabinet Folders*

To create a folder, follow these steps:

1. If you want to create a folder that extends directly from the Cabinet folder, highlight the Cabinet folder. (If you want to create a subfolder under another folder, select the folder under which you want to create the subfolder.) You can also highlight the Work In Progress folder to create subfolders underneath it.

2. Choose File → New → Folder.

TIP

> You can right mouse click the folder and choose New Folder from the QuickMenu.

3. Select the type of folder you want to create from the list: Personal, Shared, or Find Results and click Next.

4. Enter the folder name that describes the folder. You can use the Position area at the bottom of the dialog box to place the folder where you'd like it, as shown in Figure 4.10.

TIP

> If you want to move a folder later, simply click it from the main screen and drag it to where you want it.

5. Click Next to continue creating the folder. You will see the settings dialog screen, as shown in Figure 4.11.

F I G U R E   4.10   *Creating a New Folder*

6. You can change the description, item source and type, default view and sort, and the column information for the folder. Once you have personalized these choices, you can save them by clicking the Save As button and naming it.

FIGURE 4.11
New Folder Settings

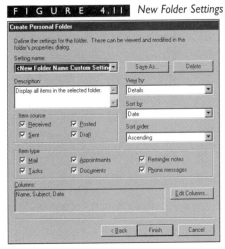

You can choose from a list of predefined folder settings in the Setting Name drop-down list.

TIP

7. If you are creating a Personal Folder, click Finish to create the folder. (Shared Folders are discussed later in this chapter.)

8. If you are creating a Find Results folder, you will see the Find dialog box, as discussed earlier in this chapter. Enter the Find criteria and click Finish to create the Find Results Folder.

As you create folders, you can change the settings later by editing the properties of the folder. Highlight the folder, click the right mouse button and choose Properties.

We explain more about how to customize the Cabinet and its folders in Chapter 10.

NOTE

To delete a folder:

1. Select the folder to be deleted.

2. Choose Edit → Delete. (Alternatively, you can right-click the folder and choose Delete from the QuickMenu.) A summary of the messages in the folder will appear, as shown in Figure 4.12.

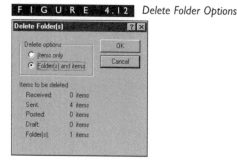

F I G U R E   4.12   *Delete Folder Options*

3. Choose whether to delete only the messages or both the folder and its messages.

4. Choose OK.

To rename a folder:

1. Select the folder to be renamed, right-click it, and then choose Rename from the QuickMenu.

2. Edit the folder name and press Enter.

TIP

You can use the Folders option under the Edit menu to determine which folders open in the main GroupWise screen when you start GroupWise. You can also use this dialog box to move folders up or down in the listing of folders, create new folders, and rename folders as shown in Figure 4.13.

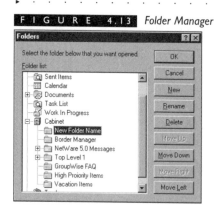

F I G U R E   4.13   *Folder Manager*

Managing Messages Using Folders

There are two different ways that you can place a message in a folder: by moving it there or by linking it to the folder. When you move a message to a folder, the message is actually stored in that folder.

To move a message into a folder, do the following:

1. Expand folders (if necessary) by clicking the button with a plus sign (+) to the left of the folder. The target folder needs to appear in the folder tree.

2. Click the message in the Items Area and drag it into the target folder. The message is now stored in that folder. If the message was previously stored in a different folder, it no longer appears there.

When you link a message to a folder, a copy of the message is placed in the destination folder. Once this is done, you can see the message in the original folder and in the folder to which the message has been linked. Any modifications to the original message (for example, changes in the appearance of the message icon) will be reflected in the folder to which the message has been linked.

Follow these steps to link a message to a folder:

1. If necessary, expand folders by clicking the plus sign to the left of the folders.

2. Hold down the Ctrl key on your keyboard, click the message, and drag it from the original folder into the target folder. The message is now stored in both the original folder and the folder to which the message has been linked.

You can also use the dialog box shown in Figure 4.14 to move and link your messages to folders. To access this dialog box, highlight a message and choose the Move / Link Selections to Folders option under the Edit menu.

FIGURE 4.14 *Moving and Linking Messages to Folders*

Using Message Threading in a Folder

When you use message threading, you can view the whole history of messages and replies behind a particular message. Message threading has many uses: You can follow workflow as it develops. You can also go back and review certain steps in a long process. Figure 4.15 shows message threading.

To enable message threading in a folder:

I. Open a folder by clicking it.

2. Click View → Display Settings → Discussion Threads.

Now you will see all of the messages and their replies in a particular folder.

TIP Message threading is particularly useful when viewing Discussions in a Shared Folder. Shared Folders are next in this chapter, and Discussions are covered in Chapter 7.

F I G U R E   4.15 *Message Threads*

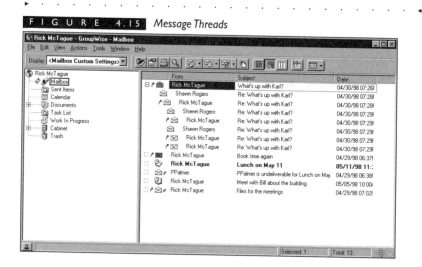

Sharing Folders

When you create a folder in GroupWise 5, you can easily share it (and its contents) with other people in your system. This feature, called shared folders, is an excellent way to manage information that pertains to many people. For example, your company might have a shared folder, called Company Notices, to store messages intended for the entire company.

As mentioned before, access to a shared folder is controlled by the creator of the folder. In the Company Notices example, a few key people might receive

Add privileges (to add messages to the folder) and everyone else would be given Read privileges. Table 4.1 explains the different kinds of access privileges.

TABLE 4.1	Access Privileges
ACCESS PRIVILEGE	**DESCRIPTION**
Read	View and read messages in a folder
Add	Add messages to a folder
Edit	Modify items in a folder
Delete	Delete items from a folder

To share a folder:

1. Highlight the folder you would like to share. (If you select a folder that has subordinate folders, only the selected folder will be shared not the folders underneath it.)

2. Choose Sharing from the File menu. The Sharing tab opens, and the Not Shared option is highlighted. Alternatively, right mouse click and choose Sharing from the Quick Menu.

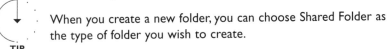

TIP When you create a new folder, you can choose Shared Folder as the type of folder you wish to create.

3. Select Shared With and enter the names of the users you would like to share the folder with, or click the browse button next to the Users field to open the Address Book. If you open the Address Book, double-click the users you wish to share this folder with. Choose View and then Filter for Groups if you want to share the folder with a group. (If you choose a group, you will be sharing with all members of the group. You can set the permissions for each person as described below.) Choose OK.

4. From the Sharing properties page, highlight a user from the list (or select multiple users with either Shift-click or Ctrl-click) and choose the access privileges you want the person to have. All users added to the Sharing list receive Read access by default. (Modify enables users to change the items in the folder, and Delete enables users to erase items from the folder.)

5. Choose OK.

6. A Shared Folder Notification screen appears. All new participants are displayed, and a mini message screen appears. Fill in the subject line, enter a short message, and choose OK.

Your Shared Folder Notification message will automatically be sent to the participants, informing them about their access to the shared folder. The people you shared the folder with will receive a "Shared Folder Notification" message in their mailbox. Each recipient will need to "install" the Shared Folder. To install a Shared Folder:

1. Double-click the Shared Folder Notification message in your mailbox folder. You'll see the Install Shared Folder wizard start (see Figure 4.16).

2. Read the summary information and note the rights that you have been granted to this Shared Folder. Click Next.

3. The Install Shared Folder screen lets you name the folder whatever you'd like, and place it in your individual structure of folders wherever you'd like. Use the Up, Down, Right, and Left buttons to move the folder. Click Finish to install the Shared Folder.

TIP When you install a shared folder from someone else, the Shared Folder is represented by a hand with a red (Novell Red) sleeve pointing to the left (your folders). If you create a folder, the sleeve is blue, and is pointing toward the right (items).

F I G U R E   4 . 1 6   *Shared Folder Notification*

TIP

WiseGuide: You can use shared folders to move mail from one user to another. This would be useful for directly exchanging a large group of messages, rather than forwarding them individually. Following are the steps involved. For this example we will define the Source User as the one whose mail is to be moved, and the Target User as the user who is to become the new "owner" of that mail:

1. The Source User shares a folder, or folders, containing the mail to be moved. The Target User is added to the access list and granted all rights.

2. The Target User accepts the shared folder or folders.

3. The Target User drags all items from these shared folders to other folders in his own mailbox.

4. After waiting for the move-to-folder operation to complete (usually just a minute or two), the Target User deletes the shared folders.

5. The Source User may now delete the shared folders. Note that when the Source User looks in these folders (before deleting them), all of the items in them are gone.

Using Filters to Manage Your Messages

You can use filters to screen out certain messages when viewing messages in any GroupWise folder. For example, you can apply a filter to your Mailbox that displays only your Mail and Phone messages, or a filter that displays only your unopened messages. You can save the filters you create and use them again later.

Here are some situations in which a filter can be very useful:

▶ You have a lot of messages in your Mailbox, and you want to see only unopened messages.

▶ You want to see only messages that were received during a specific period of time (for example, from January 1, 1996 to February 1, 1996).

▶ You want to see only messages you received from a specific person.

▶ You want to see only high-priority messages.

▶ You want to see only messages that contain a certain keyword in the Subject: field.

NOTE

A filter does not remove messages from your Mailbox; it only determines which messages are displayed. When you close a filtered display, the filter is automatically removed. The next time you open the same folder, all of the messages appear again. The exception to this is if you used a filter from the predefined list of filters. In such a case, the filter stays active.

Filter Terminology

There are five key terms you should understand before you begin working with filters:

- Filter topic
- Filter qualifier
- Filter variable/constant
- Filter group
- Filter terminator

Filter Topic

The filter topic is the part (or parts) of a message you want considered when GroupWise determines which messages to display. The following list shows the various filter topics from which you can choose:

- Annotation
- Assigned Date
- Attachment List
- Attachments
- Author
- BC:
- Caller's Company
- Caller's Name
- Caller's Phone Number
- CC:
- Copy Type
- Created
- Date Opened
- Delivered

- Document Created Date
- Document Creator
- Document Number
- Document Type
- Due / End Date
- Filename Extension
- From:
- Item Source
- Item Status
- Item Type
- Library
- Message
- Number Accepted
- Number Deleted

- ▸ Number Completed
- ▸ Number Opened
- ▸ Number Replied
- ▸ Opened By
- ▸ Place
- ▸ Posted By
- ▸ Priority
- ▸ Send Options
- ▸ Size
- ▸ Started
- ▸ Subclass

- ▸ Subject:
- ▸ Task Category
- ▸ Task Priority
- ▸ To:
- ▸ Total Recipients
- ▸ Version Created Date
- ▸ Version Creator
- ▸ Version Description
- ▸ Version Number
- ▸ Version Status
- ▸ View Name

Filter Qualifier

The filter qualifier is the logic component of a filter; it indicates the selections to be made. Each filter topic will have a different list of available qualifiers. For example, Less Than applies to the filter topic Size, while Begins With is applicable to the filter topic From, but not to Size.

The following list shows the different filter qualifiers:

- ▸ Contains
- ▸ Begins With
- ▸ Matches
- ▸ Includes
- ▸ Does Not Include
- ▸ Equal To
- ▸ Not Equal To
- ▸ Less Than
- ▸ Less Than or Equal To
- ▸ Greater Than
- ▸ Greater Than or Equal To
- ▸ Equal To Field
- ▸ Not Equal To Field
- ▸ Less Than Field

- ▸ Less Than or Equal to Field
- ▸ Greater Than Field
- ▸ Greater Than or Equal to Field
- ▸ On
- ▸ Before
- ▸ On or After
- ▸ After
- ▸ On or After Date
- ▸ On or Before
- ▸ On Date
- ▸ On or Before Date
- ▸ After Date
- ▸ Before Date

Filter Variable/Constant

A filter variable is the input on which GroupWise bases message filtering, such as a user's name. A filter constant sets the parameters of the filter topic. For example, High is a filter constant for the filter topic Priority; Phone Message is a filter constant for the filter topic Item Type.

Filter Group

A filter group is a single, complete decision line in one filter. The formula for filter groups is explained in the section, "Building a Filter."

Filter Terminator

The filter terminator determines what kind of action GroupWise will take once it has made the proper selections. Table 4.2 explains the different filter terminators available.

TABLE 4.2	Filter Terminators
TERMINATOR	**ACTION**
And	Adds an "And" condition to a single filter group
Or	Adds an "Or" condition to a single filter group
Insert Row	Adds an additional condition row in a single filter group
Delete Row	Deletes a condition row in a single filter group
Insert Group	Adds an additional filter group
End	Terminates the filter

Building a Filter

When you build a filter, you specify the criteria GroupWise will use to determine which messages to display. The formula for this decision appears in the Build Filter dialog box, as shown in Figure 4.17.

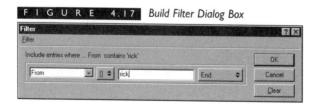

FIGURE 4.17 *Build Filter Dialog Box*

The formula for building a filter is:

```
Include entries where <Filter topic> <Qualifier>
<Variable/Constant>
```

For example, `Include entries where Item type = Phone Message` will display only Phone messages in the folder.

A simple filter is a single-decision filter. A complex filter is one where multiple decisions can be evaluated. The Filter Terminator field in the far right side of the Build Filter dialog box enables you to add more than one decision.

The filter in Figure 4.18 displays only high-priority messages received from Rick.

FIGURE 4.18 *Complex Filter*

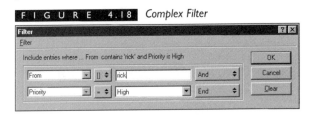

To apply a filter to a folder:

1. Open the folder, click View → Filter → Edit / Create.

2. Select the display criteria, choose Filter, and then Save (if you want to use this filter again). You will need to specify a filter name, and click the Put on menu option to add this filter to the menu.

TIP If your filter does not display any items, you will see the dialog box shown in Figure 4.19.

3. Click OK to apply the filter.

FIGURE 4.19 *Filter Feedback*

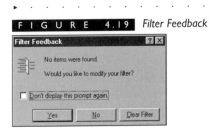

If you want to use a previously created filter:

1. Click View → Filter.

2. Select the filter you would like to use and choose OK. The folder will now display only the filtered messages.

To return to your normal, unfiltered view, right-click in the filtered folder and choose Clear Filter from the QuickMenu.

You can use filters to locate messages. For example, if you know that John Smith sent you a message, but you can't find it among your many messages, create a filter that screens out all messages except those from John Smith.

Managing Your Outgoing Messages

The Sent Items folder is a Find folder that automatically searches for all messages you have sent, regardless of the personal folder you filed them in. You retain access to these messages for three purposes: to track the status of the message, to edit and resend the message, and to retract the message.

Checking the Status of Sent Items

GroupWise offers the distinctive feature of tracking the status of sent messages. With status messages, you can find out the disposition of any message you have sent.

You can get some information about the message simply by looking at the icon to the left of the message in the Sent Items folder. For example, if the item has not been opened by the recipient, the envelope will be closed. If the recipient has opened the message, the envelope icon is open.

Table 4.3 shows the various icons that may appear next to items in the Sent Items folder.

T A B L E 4.3	*Sent Items Icons*
ICON	**DESCRIPTION**
🙁	This icon indicates that GroupWise could not deliver the item to one or more recipients.
⊠	Next to a Task, this icon indicates that at least one recipient deleted the Task without marking it complete. Next to an Appointment, the icon indicates that at least one recipient deleted or declined the Appointment without accepting it.

ICON	DESCRIPTION	
	Next to an Appointment, this icon means that not every recipient has accepted the Appointment. Next to a Task, the icon means that not every recipient has completed the Task.	

The status messages in GroupWise correspond to specific message types. For example, you can check to see if a Phone message has been read or if a Task you sent has been completed. However, you can't see if an e-mail message has been completed because you can only mark a Task Completed. Table 4.4 lists the different status messages, and Table 4.5 shows the different status messages that correspond to each message type.

TABLE 4.4	*Description of Status Messages*
STATUS	**DESCRIPTION**
Delivered	The message has been delivered to the recipient's Mailbox.
Replied	The message has been replied to by the recipient.
Opened	The message has been opened by the recipient.
Retracted	The message has been retracted from the recipient's mailbox.
Deleted	The message has been moved to the recipient's Trash.
Emptied	The message has been purged from the recipient's Trash.
Completed	The Task has been completed.
Accepted	The Appointment, Note, or Task has been accepted by the recipient.
Declined	The Appointment, Note, or Task has been declined by the recipient.
Downloaded	The message has been downloaded by a remote client.
Transferred	The message has been transferred to the gateway.

TABLE 4.5 *Message Type/Status Message Correspondence*

MESSAGE TYPE STATUS	E-mail Message	Phone Message	Meeting Request	Task Assignment	Reminder Note
Delivered	✔	✔	✔	✔	✔
Replied	✔	✔	✔	✔	✔
Opened	✔	✔	✔	✔	✔
Retracted	✔	✔	✔	✔	✔
Deleted	✔	✔	✔	✔	✔
Emptied	✔	✔	✔	✔	✔
Completed				✔	
Accepted			✔	✔	✔
Declined			✔	✔	✔
Downloaded	✔	✔	✔	✔	✔
Transferred	✔	✔	✔	✔	✔

To check the status of a message:

1. Click the Sent Items folder.

2. Double-click the message for which you want the status. (Alternatively, you can select a message, right-click it, and choose Properties from the QuickMenu.)

Figure 4.20 shows a typical message with a status indicator.

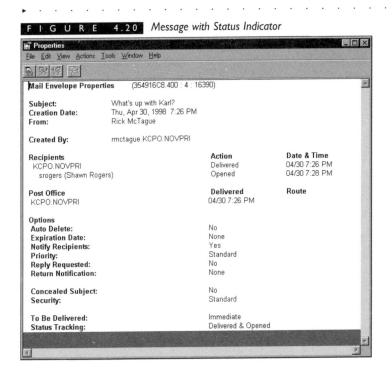

FIGURE 4.20 *Message with Status Indicator*

Retracting Messages

Retracting a message is extremely useful if you have regrets about a sent message, or you would otherwise like to *pull back* a message you have sent. As long as the message has not been opened, you can retract it.

NOTE You cannot retract messages sent through a gateway to another mail system, such as messages you send to Internet users. You can only retract a message through a gateway if the recipient's system is GroupWise.

To retract a message:

1. Click the Sent Items folder.

2. Click the message you want to retract and press the Delete key, or choose Edit and then Delete. (As a shortcut, right-click a message and choose Delete from the QuickMenu.)

3. From the Delete Item dialog box, shown in Figure 4.21, make a choice about which Mailboxes you want to remove the message from:

   • My Mailbox will remove the message from your Sent Items folder only, leaving a copy in the recipient's Mailbox.

   • Recipient's Mailbox will remove the message from all recipients' Mailboxes, leaving a copy in your Sent Items folder.

   • All Mailboxes will remove the message from all recipients' Mailboxes as well as from your Sent Items folder.

4. Click OK and the message will be retracted.

FIGURE 4.21 *Retracting a Message*

NOTE You can only retract a message if it has not been opened by the recipient. The Delete from Recipient's Mailbox option is the safest way to retract because you still keep a copy of the item in your Sent Items folder (for status tracking, resending, and so on).

Resending Messages

If you have ever sent a message to the president of your company only to read it later and find a glaring typo, you'll appreciate being able to resend messages with GroupWise. From the Sent Items folder, you can edit a message you have sent and resend it — with an option to retract the original message.

To resend a message:

1. Click the Sent Items folder.

2. Click the message you want to edit, choose Actions, and select Resend. (As a shortcut, right-click a message and choose Resend from the QuickMenu.)

3. Edit the message, click the Send button, and answer Yes when you are prompted with the Retract Original Item? Dialog box (shown in Figure 4.22).

FIGURE 4.22
Retracting the Original Message when Resending

Managing the Trash

Do you know someone who likes to keep everything, supposing that "someday he might need it" — only to clutter up an attic or basement? Well, GroupWise is like that. Deleted messages stick around in the Trash folder until you manually empty it, or until trash day rolls around. Trash day is set up just like it is in your neighborhood — once a week. However, you can change the default setting for emptying the Trash. (We explain how to change the default setting in Chapter 10.)

You saw how to delete messages in Chapter 2. Once messages have been deleted, you can do one of two things: purge them from the Trash or undelete them.

To purge the Trash, choose Edit → Empty Trash.

To undelete a message:

1. Highlight the Trash folder. All deleted items will appear in the Items Area.

2. Select a message or group of messages from the Items Area.

3. Select Edit and Undelete. (Alternatively, right-click the message or group and choose Undelete from the QuickMenu.)

The message returns to its original location.

Summary

In this chapter, we explained how to use the message management features of GroupWise — finding, archiving, saving, and printing messages; storing messages in folders; using filters; and managing the Trash. You also learned how to manage your outgoing messages with the Sent Items folder — a feature that sets GroupWise apart from other messaging systems.

CHAPTER 5

Personal Calendaring and Task Management

In this chapter, we show you how to use GroupWise 5 to replace your old-fashioned calendar or daily planner. The time-management features of Group-Wise are extraordinarily useful. Once you start using these features, you'll wonder how you ever got by without them.

When you showed up for work this morning and turned on your computer, one of your first tasks was probably to check your e-mail. After that, you probably checked your calendar to see what appointments you had for the day. With GroupWise, the integration of the e-mail interface with your Calendar makes it very easy to do most of your communications and scheduling with one program. As you saw in Chapter 1, switching from e-mail to your Calendar is as simple as clicking the Calendar folder.

With the Calendar's built-in views you can instantly display Calendar items, such as Appointments or Tasks. Later in this chapter, you'll learn how to change your view to one that suits your needs.

In order to use the GroupWise Calendar system most effectively, you need to understand the difference between the various Calendar items. The Calendar keeps track of three different kinds of personal reminders: Posted Appointments, Reminder Notes, and Posted Tasks. Table 5.1 explains the different Calendar items.

T A B L E 5.1	Calendar Items
ITEM	**DESCRIPTION**
Posted Appointments	Personal Meetings and events on a certain date with a start time and an end time (duration)
Reminder Notes	Personal reminders for a certain date
Posted Tasks	Personal project entries with a "tickle" entry in your Calendar from the start date through the due date, with a priority level

NOTE Note the distinction between personal Calendar items (Posted) and Group Calendar items. *Posted items* are not sent to anyone; you post them to your own Calendar. *Group items* are sent to other people in much the same way you send e-mail messages. (Group calendaring is discussed in Chapter 6.)

The Calendar Interface

When you click the Calendar folder, a condensed view of your Calendar appears in the Items Area on the right side of the main GroupWise screen. This view is your Calendar folder view, as shown in Figure 5.1. Initially, all of your Calendar items — both personal and group — appear in your Calendar. Notice that there are five tabs along the top of the Calendar display: the Day, Week, Month, Year, and Multi-User.

Day View

The Calendar folder view uses a Day view to display your Appointments, Reminder Notes, and Tasks in separate panes in the items area along with a three month view. The subject line of each Calendar item appears. To remove or add an item in the Calendar folder view, simply click the heading bar button (Appointments, Reminder Notes, or Tasks) for the item.

Week View

The Week tab displays your calendar items for the entire week, as shown in Figure 5.2. Maximize GroupWise and see up to five days' worth of Calendar information at once in the Week Calendar folder view. You can add or subtract days from the listing by clicking the plus (+) or minus (–) sign in the top-right corner of the display. You can also navigate forward in the calendar by clicking the right arrow (ahead) or the left arrow (back). You can click the Appointments, Reminder Notes, or Tasks buttons to change the displayed items.

F I G U R E   5 . 1   *Calendar Folder View*

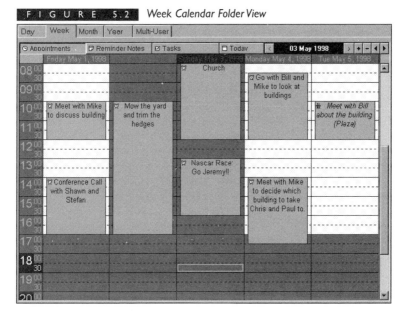

FIGURE 5.2 *Week Calendar Folder View*

TIP

Leave your mouse pointer over a calendar item to see a quick view of the details of the item.

Month View

The Month tab displays your calendar items for the entire month, as shown in Figure 5.3. You can use the arrows at the top-right corner of the display to change the month. Notice that the month and year are displayed. You can use the Appointments, Reminder Notes, and Tasks buttons to change what information is displayed in the month view.

TIP

Right-click any day to create a new calendar item quickly. You can also double-click any day to see a larger display for that date. Right-click any day in the Month view and choose Show Item icons to see the symbols next to the items. Choose Show Appt. Durations to display the hours and minutes for each appointment.

◀

F I G U R E   5 . 3   *Month Calendar Folder View*

| Day | Week | Month | Year | Multi-User |

| ⊙ Appointments | 🗐 Reminder Notes | ☑ Tasks | □ Today | ‹ | **May 1998** | › |

Sunday	Monday	Tuesday	Wednesday	Thursday	Friday	Saturday
26	27	28	29	30	1 Meet with Mike to d Conference Call wit • Pick up snacks fo □ Work on Chapter	2 Mow the yard and
3 Church Nascar Race: Go J	4 Go with Bill and Mik Meet with Mike to c	5 *Meet with Bill abou*	6	7	8	9
10	11 *Lunch on May 11* • Chris and Paul he	12 Meet with Novell	13	14 • Chris and Paul lea	15	16
17	18 • Go to Vienna	19 • Go to Vienna	20 • Go to Vienna	21 • Go to Vienna	22 • Go to Vienna	23
24	25	26	27 • Richard's at World	28 • Alison and Beth g	29 • Alison and Beth g	30 • Alison and Beth g
31	1	2	3	4	5	6

Year View

The Year tab enables you to see an entire year's worth of items, as shown in Figure 5.4. Note that days that in boldface are days for which you have calendar items set. You can use the arrows next to the year to change the year being displayed.

TIP

Double-click any day in the Year view to see details about that day.

Multi-User View

The Multi-User calendar tab is used to view more than one person's calendar information at a time. We cover the Multi-User calendar in Chapter 6.

FIGURE 5.4 *Year Calendar Folder View*

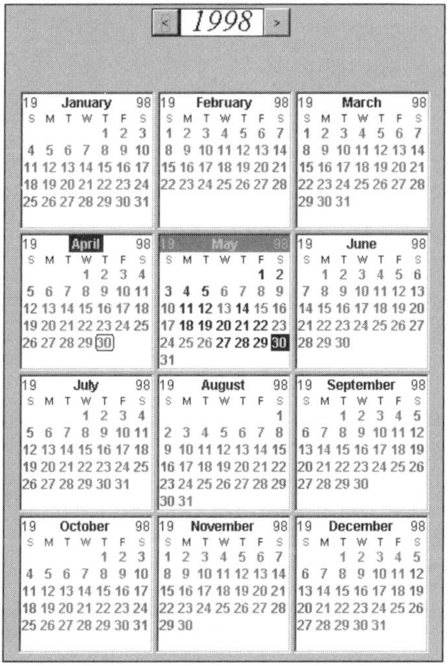

Changing Views

From any of these views, if you want to see the Calendar items for a different day, select View → Go to Date. Type the desired date on the date line, click the date in the month displayed, or scroll forward or back one month (single arrows), forward or back a year (double arrows) until the desired month and day is displayed. Figure 5.5 shows the Go to Date dialog box.

To return to the current day's Calendar items quickly, click the View menu and choose Go to Today. The Week, Month, and Multi-User views have a Go to Today button on the heading bar.

FIGURE 5.5 *Go to Date*

TIP

If you have enabled the QuickViewer, the message contents of each Calendar item will appear in the QuickViewer pane at the bottom of the screen.

In addition to the Calendar folder views previously discussed, you can choose from 15 different views of the Calendar, including the Calendar folder view. Table 5.2 lists the different Calendar views. You'll want to experiment with them until you find the one that best suits your work style.

TABLE 5.2 *Calendar Views*

NAME	FEATURES
Day	Displays Appointments, Reminder Notes, and Tasks three months at a time
Week	Displays Appointments, Reminder Notes, and Tasks five to seven days at a time
Week & Calendar	Displays Appointments, Reminder Notes, and Tasks five to seven days at a time with month at a glance
Month Displays	Displays Appointments, Reminder Notes, and Tasks a month at a time
Month & Calendar	Displays Appointments, Reminder Notes, and Tasks a month at a time with several months at a glance
Year	Displays the entire year. Boldface dates on the Calendar contain scheduled items, as shown in Figure 5.3
Desk Calendar	Displays daily Appointments and Tasks one month at a time
Notebook	Displays Reminder Notes and Tasks for one day

NAME	FEATURES
Day Projects	Displays expanded Cabinet folders, Group Appointments, Tasks, and Reminder Notes — three months at a glance
Day Planner	Displays Tasks, Appointments, and Reminder Notes — four months at a glance
Project Planner	Displays Tasks and Reminder Notes — all folders expanded, four months at a glance, as shown in Figure 5.6
Appt	Displays Appointments for one day
Note	Displays Reminder Notes for one day
Task	Displays Tasks for one day
Multi-User	Displays Appointments, Reminder Notes, and Tasks for multiple users

F I G U R E   5 . 6   *Project Planner Calendar View*

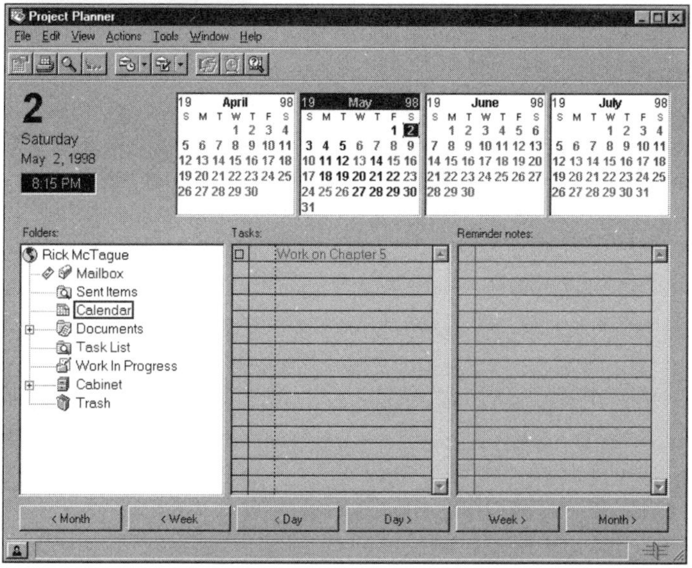

To open a Calendar view:

1. Find the Calendar View button at the right-hand side of the Toolbar. If the Toolbar is not visible, select View → Toolbar.

> If your desired view is set as the default Calendar View, simply click the Calendar View button on the Toolbar and your view
> **TIP** will be displayed.

2. Left-click the down arrow next to the button to see a list of all 15 views. Move your mouse to the desired view and left-click again.

> **WiseGuide:** Once you have found a view that you like, you can set it as the default by selecting Tools → Options. If you like to use different Calendar views at different times, add the Calendar
> **TIP** button to your Toolbar. The Calendar button provides you with one-click access to any of the Calendar views. (Setting default options and customizing the Toolbar is explained in Chapter 10.)

To change your Calendar view:

1. Choose Edit → Change To → More.

2. Select a view from the list and click OK.

Task List

The Task List folder contains a list of your Tasks — both posted and group. The Task List is a handy feature because you can see all of your Tasks in one place; you don't have to scan through the entire Calendar to locate them.

Notice in Figure 5.7 that you can see each Task's priority level and due date. Also note the different icons for incomplete Tasks and completed Tasks.

F I G U R E   5 . 7   Task List

Creating Posted Appointments

A large part of time management involves scheduling appointments, and GroupWise provides an easy-to-use interface for creating and managing your personal engagements. Posted Appointment messages only appear on your Calendar; you don't send them to other people. Figure 5.8 shows an example of a Posted Appointment.

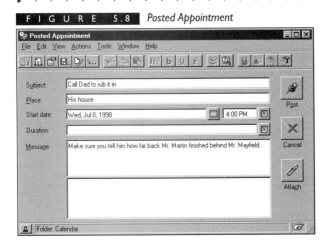

F I G U R E   5.8   *Posted Appointment*

As you can see in Figure 5.8, a Posted Appointment includes the following information: appointment date, start time, duration, and place. The time increment (default of 15 minutes) can be changed, as well as the date format. You can customize GroupWise to use military date and time as well as other formats. (See Chapter 10 for more information on customizing your GroupWise environment.) The subject line of an Appointment appears in the Calendar.

To create a Posted Appointment:

1. Click the down arrow next to the Appointment button on the Toolbar and choose Posted Appointment from the list. Alternatively, in the Calendar view double-click the time for which you want to make the Posted Appointment and you will achieve the same result.

2. Enter a subject line for the Appointment and place more detailed information in the message area.

3. Fill in the Appointment date, start time, and duration, and choose Post to add the Appointment to your Calendar.

You can also set alarms for your Appointments. To set an alarm:

1. Select an Appointment and then right-click it.

2. Choose Set Alarm from the QuickMenu. You'll see the Set Alarm dialog box, shown in Figure 5.9.

3. Specify, in hours and minutes, how much advance notice you want. The maximum is 99 hours and 59 minutes. You can also set up a variety of sounds for the alarm. (See Chapter 10 for information on how to customize the alarm.)

4. Click OK. Notice the alarm clock icon next to the Appointment.

F I G U R E 5 . 9 *Set Alarm Dialog Box*

Once you set an alarm, you can change the time and remove it by clicking the Clear button.

TIP

Creating Posted Tasks

Posted Tasks are very useful, reminding you to finish assignments or projects that may last for several days. As you saw earlier in this chapter, your Posted Tasks appear in the Task List folder in the main GroupWise screen.

Each Task has a start date, an end date, and a priority level, as shown in Figure 5.10. The priority level determines the order in which the Tasks appear in the list, based on an alphabetic and numeric code. For example, a Task with a priority of A1 appears before A2, and A2 appears before B1. The code you assign to a Task is completely up to you. You can use only letters or only numbers if you prefer.

The subject line of each task you create appears on the starting day's Calendar, and will carry forward each day until you mark the Task Completed checkbox. If a Task is not marked completed by the due date, it will continue to be carried forward, but it will appear red in the Task List.

To create a Posted Task:

1. Click the arrow next to the Task button on the Toolbar and choose Posted Task from the list.

TIP

You can also double-click in the Task area of your calendar to create a new Posted Task.

2. Enter a subject line for the task. You can place more detailed information in the message area.

3. Enter a priority level for the task (or leave the priority setting blank if you like).

4. Enter a start date (which must be today's date or later) and an end date.

5. Choose Post to enter the Task in your Calendar.

To mark a task completed, click the Task heading button in the Calendar folder. Click the box next to the task in the Task list. Notice that a check mark appears in the box. The new task also appears in the Task List folder.

Creating Reminder Notes

Reminder Notes can be added to your Calendar and tied to certain dates as reminders, as shown in Figure 5.11. The subject line of each Note appears in your Calendar. You can use Reminder Notes to remind yourself about anything you like — for example, picking up your dry cleaning. You might also use a recurring note to mark paydays on your Calendar.

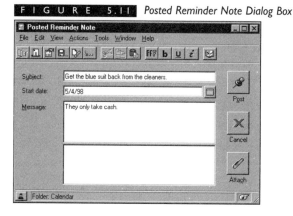

F I G U R E   5.11 *Posted Reminder Note Dialog Box*

To create a Reminder Note:

1. Click the Reminder Notes heading button in the Calendar folder, and then double-click the Note pane under your Appointments.

2. Enter a subject line for the Note. If you like, you can place details about the Note in the message area.

3. Fill in the date for the Note and choose OK to add the note to your Calendar.

Rescheduling Appointments, Tasks, and Reminder Notes

Rescheduling an Appointment, Task, or Reminder Note only requires a simple click and drag of the mouse.

To move an Appointment, Task, or Reminder Note to a different day:

1. Open your Calendar folder.

2. If the day you need to move the item to does not appear, use either the Week or Month tab on the Calendar folder view, or open the Day view of the Calendar. (See the "Calendar Views" section at the beginning of this chapter for instructions on changing views.) The Day view displays three months at a glance.

3. Click the Appointment, Task, or Reminder note you want to reschedule and drag it to the new day.

To change the time of a Posted Appointment:

1. Open your Calendar folder and single-click the Appointment you want to change.

2. With the mouse button held down, drag the Appointment to a new time on the same day, and the Appointment will move.

Calendar Item "Morphing"

Suppose you are over halfway finished with a new Posted Appointment only to realize that you should be making a Posted Task instead. Instead of canceling and starting over, you can invoke GroupWises' powerful "morphing" feature. This feature lets you change one message type to another, on the fly. For example, you can keep all of the information about the appointment (subject, message body, and so on). and change it into a new task, retaining all of the information.

There are two ways to change a calendar item from one type to another:

▸ **Method 1 (best to use after the item has been created):** Click the calendar item and drag it to another area in the Calendar display. For example, you could click a Post Appointment and drag it to the Task area and the item will change to a Post Task.

▸ **Method 2 (best to use while the item is being created):** Anytime you create a new calendar item, click the Change Item Type button on the Toolbar (it has an arrow with two dots). You will see the Change To dialog box shown in Figure 5.12.

Click the desired new calendar item type and choose OK. The screen will change to the new item type.

TIP Notice that when you use Method 1, the mouse pointer changes to represent what you are doing, using the item icons with an arrow in between.

FIGURE 5.12
Change to Dialog Box

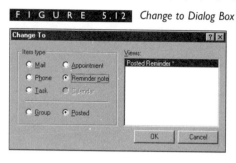

You can also use the Edit → Change To menu option to change the item type.

TIP

Summary

In this chapter, you have seen the many features of GroupWise as they relate to your own calendar. The Posted Appointments, Reminder Notes, and Posted Tasks that you create to manage your time can also be used to invite people to meetings, remind them of events on a certain day, and to delegate tasks. The next chapter shows you how to make the most of the GroupWise 5 group scheduling and work flow features.

CHAPTER 6

Group Calendaring and
Task Management

In Chapter 5, you learned how to manage your personal Calendar items, such as Appointments and Tasks. In Chapter 6, we show you how to use the GroupWise 5 workgroup features, including group calendaring and task management.

Scheduling Meetings

When you want to schedule a meeting with other people, you send an Appointment message.

NOTE

Appointment messages that you send to other people are sometimes referred to as Meetings or Meeting Requests.

In some cases you may need to schedule a meeting for someone else, such as your supervisor. GroupWise enables you to schedule meetings for others (in other words, meetings that you don't plan to attend).

You can use the GroupWise Proxy feature to view and manage others' Calendars. (Chapter 7 explains the Proxy feature.)

Sending Appointments

You send Appointments to other GroupWise users to schedule meetings — either for yourself or for someone else. When you want to send an Appointment, you must set a start date, a start time, and a duration — just like you do for Posted (Personal) Appointments. The only difference is that you are sending the Appointment request to others, not just adding the Appointment to your Calendar.

To create and send an Appointment:

1. Click File → New → Appointment.

2. Address the Appointment message just as you would any other type of GroupWise message — by entering the names in the To: field or by using the Address Book. If you plan to attend the meeting, make sure you include your own name in the To: field. If you do not include your own name, the Appointment will not appear in your Calendar. (By default, GroupWise inserts your name in the To: field when you create an Appointment.)

3. Enter the location of the meeting in the Place: field.

TIP
If your system administrator has made the meeting place (for example, a certain conference room) a resource, you can schedule the room at the same time you send the Appointment. Open the Address Book, click View → Predefined Filters → Resources. Select the room from the list of resources. If the room has not been defined as a resource, you can describe the meeting place in the Place: field, but the room will not be reserved by GroupWise.

4. Enter a subject in the subject line. (Be descriptive because only the subject line appears in the recipients' Calendars.)

5. Enter detailed information about the meeting in the Message: field. If you like, you can attach a file such as a meeting agenda.

6. Set the date of the meeting by typing the date in the Start Date: field or by clicking the small calendar icon to the right of that field.

NOTE
If you want to create a recurring Appointment, you can use the Auto-Date feature, explained later in this chapter.

7. Set the time of the meeting by typing the time in the field to the right of the small calendar icon or by clicking the small clock icon next to that field.

8. Enter the duration of the meeting in the Duration: field (or set the duration by clicking the small clock icon to the right of the Duration: field).

9. Choose Send.

The Appointment appears in the recipients' Mailboxes and Calendars.

When you schedule meetings, you can use the Busy Search feature to find a time when all attendees are available. The Busy Search feature automatically sets the date, time, and duration of the meeting. Busy Searches are explained in the next section.

Busy Searching

The Busy Search feature is a very powerful GroupWise scheduling tool. You no longer need to call people in advance of a meeting to find a time when everyone can meet. GroupWise takes care of that chore for you.

To perform a Busy Search when scheduling a meeting:

1. Open a new Appointment message and use the Address Book to place the attendees' addresses in the To: field.

2. Click the Busy? button in the lower-right corner of the message box. GroupWise searches the users' Calendars and displays the Choose Appointment Time dialog box, as shown in Figure 6.1.

FIGURE 6.1 Busy Search Dialog Box Showing Individual Schedules

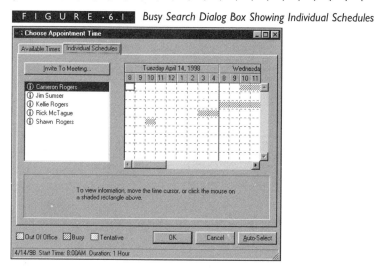

The Choose Appointment Time dialog box presents you with a grid showing you the schedule of each user you specified. An empty space across from the user name indicates that the user is available for that time.

If you want GroupWise to show you the times when all users are available, click the Available Times tab. The dialog box shown in Figure 6.2 appears.

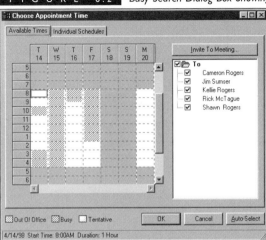

You can select the Appointment time from either of the Choose Appointment Time screens. To set the Appointment time:

1. Click the highlighted box in the grid and drag it to a time the attendees are available. You can click and drag the sides of this box to increase or decrease the duration of the meeting.

2. Click OK. The date and time of the meeting appear in the appropriate fields of the Appointment message.

Here are some handy Busy Search tips:

▶ To include more users in the Busy Search from the Choose Appointment Time dialog box, click the Invite To Meeting button.

▶ If there isn't a time when all attendees are free, you can extend the search to include more days by clicking the Invite To Meeting button and increasing the value in the Number Of Days To Search field.

▶ When the Choose Appointment Time dialog box shows that some users are busy, you can find out what a user has scheduled by clicking the box representing that time slot. (You can see the person's schedule only if the user has granted you access rights to his or her Calendar.)

▶ The Auto-Select button selects a time when all of the selected users are free for the duration you have specified.

▶ You can exclude a user from the Busy Search without removing the user from the To: field by choosing the Available Times tab and then clearing the check mark that appears next to the user's name in the right side of the dialog box. (This exclusion feature is useful when someone should be invited but it is not absolutely necessary for that person to attend.)

▶ To perform a Busy Search before creating your Appointment message, choose Tools → Busy Search. Enter the users in the dialog box that appears.

▶ You can add names to the Busy Search by clicking the Invite To Meeting button. You can delete names from the Busy Search by clicking the user name and pressing the Delete key.

▶ If you are Busy Searching for multiple users, GroupWise may take awhile to return the results on all users. You can minimize the Busy Search dialog box and work on other tasks while GroupWise receives the Busy Search results. A status box will appear on your Windows Taskbar showing you the search progress.

▶ You can do a Busy Search for a resource (such as a conference room, a company car, or a VCR) to find out times when the resource is not reserved.

To change Busy Search defaults:

1. Click Tools → Options.

2. Double-click the Date and Time icon.

3. Choose the Busy Search tab.

IMPORTANT

The Busy Search feature is only useful if all GroupWise users keep their Calendars up to date. Remember also that appointments can be delegated by recipients. Check the status of the message to see if any of the intended attendees have delegated the appointment to another person.

Sending Tasks

Use GroupWise Task messages for assigning projects to other GroupWise users. Tasks are also useful for large projects that involve many people.
To send a Task:

1. Choose File → New.
2. Select Task. The Task message shown in Figure 6.3 appears.

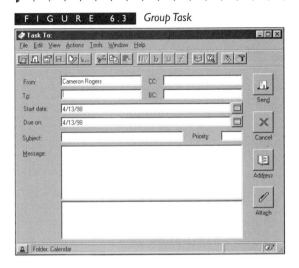

FIGURE 6.3 **Group Task**

3. Address the Task message by typing in the recipient's name or by using the Address Book.
4. Enter a priority code for the Task. The Task priority can be a character, a number, or a character followed by a number. For example, these are valid priority codes: A, B, C, 1, 2, 3, A1, B1, B2, and so on.
5. Enter the subject and message in the appropriate fields.
6. Select a start date. The start date is the date when the Task will first appear in the recipient's Calendar, after the recipient accepts the Task from his or her Mailbox.
7. Select a due date. Tasks that are not completed before the due date turn red in the recipient's Calendar.
8. Choose Send.

In addition to the priority code you enter in the Task message screen, you can also set a priority for the message:

1. Choose File.
2. Select Properties.

3. Choose the Send Options tab.

4. Select High, Normal, or Low priority from the Priority: field.

5. Choose OK.

Sending Reminder Notes

Use Reminder Notes to send reminders to people. Reminder Notes are very useful as meeting reminders because Notes appear on specific days in the recipients' Calendars. Often, Notes are used to remind others about specific assignments for upcoming meetings.

To send a Reminder Note:

I. Select File → New.

2. Select Reminder Note.

3. Enter the information in the To:, Subject:, and Message: fields.

4. Specify a date for the Note in the Start Date: field.

5. Choose Send.

Figure 6.4 shows a typical Group Note.

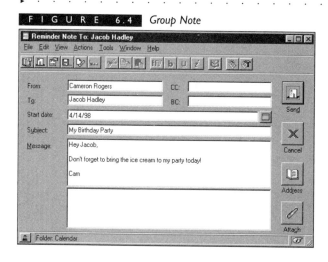

F I G U R E   6 . 4   *Group Note*

Monitoring Appointments, Tasks, and Notes

Users often fail to keep their Calendars up to date, and even though a Busy Search may show that they are available, they may not be. After you send the Appointment, you should monitor the status of the message to find out if it has been accepted, declined, or delegated (or simply ignored).

If a recipient has declined the message and has provided a comment explaining why, that comment appears in the message status information, not as a message in your Mailbox. (See Chapter 4 for more information on checking the status of sent items.)

To see whether the recipients have accepted, declined, or delegated a message, and to view their comments:

1. Open your Sent Items folder.

2. Right-click the message and choose Properties.

Retracting Appointments, Tasks, and Notes

Unlike regular e-mail messages, you can retract Appointments, Tasks, and Notes after the recipients have opened them. When you retract an Appointment, Task, or Note, it is removed from the recipients' Calendars and Mailboxes.

To retract an Appointment, Task, or Note:

1. Open your Sent Items folder and highlight the message to be retracted.

2. Press the Delete key (or right-click the message and select Delete).

3. Select Recipient's Mailbox or All Mailboxes and click OK.

To reschedule or resend a Calendar entry:

1. Right-click the message in the Sent Items folder and select Resend.

2. Change the message information, if necessary, and click Send.

3. If you want to retract the original entry, choose Yes when prompted.

Because the recipients receive no warning (the item simply disappears from their Calendars), it is good messaging etiquette to let them know you have retracted an item.

Receiving Appointments, Tasks, and Notes

The Appointments, Tasks, and Notes that you receive from other GroupWise users appear in your Mailbox along with other e-mail messages. Appointments, Tasks, and Notes also appear in your Calendar folder or in your Calendar view on the specified date. In the Calendar they appear in italics until you accept them, indicating that the item is tentative and has not been accepted.

Figure 6.5 shows an opened Calendar folder with accepted and unaccepted Appointments, Tasks, and Notes.

FIGURE 6.5 *Accepted and "Penciled-In" Calendar Entries*

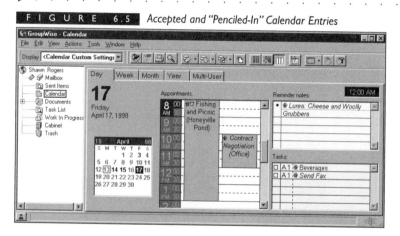

You have several options when you receive an Appointment, Task, or Note from someone else. You can accept the entry, and it will convert the tentative (italicized) entry to a regular (non-italicized) entry. Alternatively, you can decline the message, and it will move to your Trash folder.

Accepting

To accept an Appointment, Task, or Note, from the Mailbox or Calendar folder, double-click the icon to open it and choose the Accept button. Or, you can right-click the item and choose Accept from the QuickMenu.

The Accept With Options dialog box will appear which enables you to send a comment to the sender of the message. This comment will appear in the sender's message properties.

Declining

To decline an Appointment, Task, or Note, from the Mailbox or Calendar folder, double-click the icon to open it and choose the Decline button (or right-click the item and choose Decline from the QuickMenu). When you decline an entry, you are given the option to comment about why you have declined. If you enter a comment, the sender can see it when he or she checks the status of the message you declined.

Delegating

If you receive an Appointment that you cannot attend or a Task you cannot complete, but you desire that someone else attend in your place, or complete the Task, you can delegate the message.

When you delegate an Appointment or Task, you pass it along to someone else without necessarily keeping a copy for yourself. To delegate an Appointment or Task, right-click the item and choose Delegate from the QuickMenu.

To delegate an Appointment or Task when the item is open:

1. Select Actions.

2. Select Delegate. A new message is created, identical to the message you received, except that the word "Delegated" is appended to the subject line.

3. Address the message to the person to whom it is being delegated.

4. Choose Send. You will be asked if you want to keep a copy of the item in your Mailbox.

5. Answer Yes or No.

The person who sent you the message can find out that you have delegated the item by checking the message status. The "Delegated" status will appear along with the name of the person to whom you delegated the Appointment or Task.

Using Auto-Date

The GroupWise Auto-Date feature enables you to send recurring Appointments, Tasks, or Note messages. Auto-Date enables you to send one message that applies to many different days. For example, you can use an Appointment Auto-Date to schedule a staff meeting that occurs every Wednesday at 9:00 a.m. Or you can use a Task Auto-Date to make sure staff members turn in a report on a certain day each month. You can also send a Note configured with Auto-Dates to remind employees which day is payday.

There are three different ways to create Auto-Date messages:

► By Dates

► By Example

► By Formula

For the most part, the By Example method makes the By Formula method obsolete. Therefore, we do not discuss the By Formula option.

By Dates

The By Dates Auto-Date method is the easiest to use and understand. When you choose this method, a calendar opens up for the current year and you click the dates on which you want the Appointment, Task, or Note to appear. You can click the Year button to advance the calendar to the next year.

To create an Auto-Date Calendar entry using the By Dates method:

1. Open a new Appointment, Task, or Note message.

2. Fill in the To:, Subject:, and Message: fields.

3. Click the Actions pull-down menu.

4. Select Auto-Date. The Auto-Date dialog box appears, as shown in Figure 6.6. (The Dates tab is active by default.)

5. Click all dates when the Appointment, Task, or Note should appear.

6. Choose OK.

7. Choose Send to send the message.

FIGURE 6.6 *Auto-Date Dialog Box*

By Example

Use the By Example Auto-Date method when you want to send Appointments, Tasks, or Notes for dates that follow a regular pattern. For instance, a By Example Auto-Date could be used to schedule a meeting that occurs on the third Tuesday of every month.

The By Example Auto-Date requires some experimenting to get the hang of it. The following example should help you get a sense of how it works.

One of the most common ways people use Auto-Date is to create Personal Notes reminding themselves when it's payday. The following steps show how to use Auto-Date to create a Personal Note for a payday that occurs on the first and fifteenth day of every month, unless the payday falls on a weekend. If the first or fifteenth falls on a weekend, the payday occurs on the preceding Friday. Here is what you would do:

1. Click Window.

2. Click Calendar view to see your personal Calendar.

3. Double-click in the Reminder Notes field to open a new Posted Reminder Note message.

4. Click Actions.

5. Click Auto-Date.

6. Choose the Example tab.

7. In the Start: field, enter the day when the Auto-Date period should begin.

8. In the End field, enter the date when the Auto-Date period should end.

9. Click all months in the Months field to indicate that the paydays occur every month.

10. Click the drop-down list box named Days of the Week and select instead the Days of the Month setting. The dialog box changes, enabling you to specify certain days in the month for the Note.

11. Highlight Monday, Tuesday, Wednesday, Thursday, and Friday to indicate that the Note should only appear on a weekday.

12. Choose On/Before from the drop-down list located below the days you have highlighted. The On/Before option tells GroupWise that the Note can only appear on or before the day you specify. For example, if the 15th falls on a Saturday, the Note should appear on the previous Friday.

13. Click 1 and 15 in the calendar to indicate the dates when the Note should appear. Figure 6.7 shows how the Auto-Date dialog box should look at this point.

14. Click OK.

15. Fill in the remaining message fields and choose Send.

A Note will appear in your Calendar on each day that meets the Auto-Date criteria during the period you specified in the date range fields.

When you send an Appointment message or Note created using Auto-Date, one message is created and sent by the GroupWise system for every date that meets the Auto-Date criteria. If you send an Auto-Date Appointment message that occurs every Friday during a year interval, 52 separate Appointments will appear in each recipient's Mailbox. The recipient will be given the option to accept all instances at once or to accept or decline each message individually.

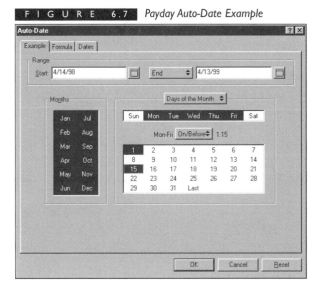

FIGURE 6.7 *Payday Auto-Date Example*

The online help system includes a guide for using the Auto-Date feature. To access the guide:

1. Click Help.

2. Click Guides.

3. Choose the GroupWise Basics option.

4. Select the "Schedule a recurring event" guide.

Multi-User Calendars

GroupWise provides for an office administrator to manage calendars for several other GroupWise users. Before you can manager another GroupWise user's calendar, the other user must give you proxy access to his or her Group-Wise calendar. The instructions for granting proxy access are provided in the next chapter.

To manage multiple users' calendars, you use the Multi-User tab that displays when you open your Calendar folder, as illustrated in Figure 6.8.

F I G U R E   6.8 *Multi-User Calendar Display*

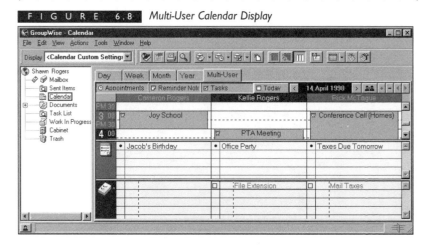

To add users to the Multi-user Calendar display:

1. Verify that the users you want to add have granted you proxy access to their calendars.

2. Click the Add User button. The Multi-User list dialog box displays (see Figure 6.9).

F I G U R E   6.9 *Multi-User List Dialog Box*

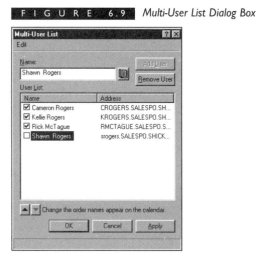

3. Enter the users' names in the Name field, or use the Address Book to select the users.

4. Click the up and down arrow buttons to change the order in which the users display in the Calendar.

5. Click OK.

TIP

You can alter the Multi-User Calendar display by clicking the message type buttons that appear directly below the tabs. You can choose to display any combination of multiple users' Appointments, Reminder Notes, and Tasks. You can also choose the order in which the tabs appear in your Calendar view by right-clicking the tabs and choosing Properties.

Calendar Printing

GroupWise provides powerful Calendar printing capabilities. You can choose from several popular formats, including formats familiar to users of the Franklin Quest day planners.

To print your GroupWise calendar:

1. Open the Calendar folder in the main GroupWise screen.

2. Click File.

3. Click Print Calendar. The dialog box shown in Figure 6.10 appears.

FIGURE 6.10 *Print Calendar Dialog Box*

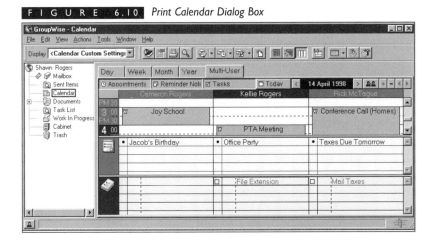

4. In the Calendar Type drop-down list box, select the printing format you prefer. The options are GroupWise, Franklin Quest, Multi-user, and text. (You should look at the formats of each option to find one that you prefer.)

5. Click the Format tab and choose the formatting options you prefer. Among the options you can select are headers, footers, and page numbers.

6. Select the Options tab, and choose the options you prefer. (Depending on the calendar type you have selected, the Options tab will provide GroupWise Options, Franklin Quest options, Multi-User options, or Text options.)

7. Click Print when done.s

Figure 6.11 shows the preview screen for the popular Franklin Quest day-planning calendar printing format.

F I G U R E   6 . 1 1 *Franklin Quest Calendar Print Preview*

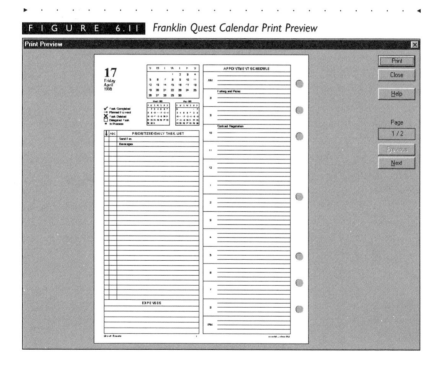

Summary

In this chapter you learned how to use the powerful GroupWise group-calendaring and task-management features.

In Chapter 7, you learn about some of the advanced workgroup features that will increase your ability to collaborate with others using GroupWise.

CHAPTER 7

Advanced Features

In this chapter, we introduce you to the advanced features of GroupWise: rules, proxies, sending options, discussions, and message threads. We also explain how to modify the look of your messages — by changing the font, text color, and text attributes — and how to embed OLE objects in messages. We will also cover a new utility called Date Difference.

Rules enable you to automate your message management. With rules, you can have GroupWise perform a wide variety of tasks automatically, such as replying to or forwarding messages, accepting appointments, and moving messages into designated folders.

With the *Proxy* feature, you can view other people's messages or calendar information (provided you have been granted the necessary rights) or enable coworkers to enter appointments into your own calendar.

Much like you can choose next-day or second-day delivery for a package, or a delivery receipt for a certified letter, you can specify many *sending options* for your GroupWise messages. In addition, you can alter the appearance of messages by adjusting fonts, color, and attributes to express your personality through your e-mail.

The *Discussions* feature adds a very productive work flow capability to GroupWise. A discussion is used to gather related messages in one area and share them with a group of people (through shared folders). The progression of messages can be viewed as a thread in the Discussion Area, like an Internet bulletin board. *Message Threads* enable you to view messages that fall in a certain place in an entire discussion.

You'll learn how to create messages that activate: Imagine creating a message that says "Click here to update your sales spreadsheet." In the center of the message is a large button that, when clicked, automatically copies an updated spreadsheet to the recipient's hard drive. Adding *OLE objects* to your messages enables you to do this and more. Finally, we cover a new utility, called *Date Difference*, that quickly calculates the number of days within a range.

Automating GroupWise with Rules

GroupWise is capable of managing most of your messages for you (even while you are not logged into the system) through GroupWise *rules*. Rules enable you to move messages to folders, generate automatic replies, forward messages, and delete messages. You can also set up rules to manage your calendar items automatically. For example, you can create a rule that accepts all the tasks your boss sends you (always a good idea) or that automatically declines appointments scheduled after 5:00 p.m. (an even better idea).

In this chapter, we won't try to list all of the possible rules you can create, but we will explain the basics for setting up rules. We'll also show you a few useful examples.

To create a rule:

1. Select Tools → Rules → New. The Rules dialog box shown in Figure 7.1 appears.

2. Fill in the fields and choose Save.

The sample rule created in Figure 7.1 moves all High Priority messages to a folder named Important Items.

F I G U R E   7.1   *The Rules Dialog Box*

The rule is added to your *Rule List* and is automatically activated. (The red check mark in the box next to a rule indicates that the rule is activated.) Your Rule List shows all of the rules you have saved — both active and inactive, as shown in Figure 7.2.

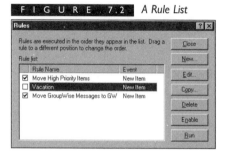

FIGURE 7.2 A Rule List

- **To modify a rule**: Click the rule and then the Edit button. You can then change any of the parameters of the rule. Choose Save to complete your changes to the rule.

- **To copy or delete a rule**: Click the rule and then choose either the Copy button or the Delete button. You can use the Copy feature to create additional rules, based on the original rule. For example, if you create a rule that routes all message from a specific user to a specific folder, you could copy this rule for messages from another user that you want routed to a different folder (without having to create a new rule from scratch).

- **To activate or deactivate a rule**: Click the checkbox next to the rule or use the Enable/Disable button to the right of the Rule List.

- **To run a rule**: Click the rule in the list and then click the Run button. You need to use the Run button only when you create a new rule that acts upon messages already in your Mailbox.

TIP

Your Rules are executed in the order in which they appear in the Rules List (refer to Figure 7.2). This is important when, for example, you have a delete rule before a reply rule. To change the order in which the rules are executed, click a rule in the Rules list dialog box and drag it to a new position.

Figures 7.3 through 7.5 show the details of three commonly used rules:

- A vacation rule that will automatically reply to the sender and forward the message to someone

- A rule that automatically accepts Appointments from a certain person

- A rule that moves messages to a folder automatically, based on the subject of the message

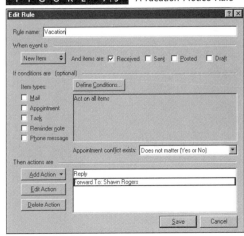

FIGURE 7.3 *A Vacation Notice Rule*

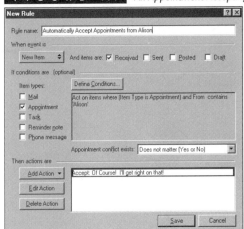

FIGURE 7.4 *An Appointment-Accepting Rule*

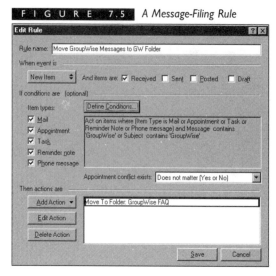

F I G U R E   7.5   A Message-Filing Rule

TIP

To create this rule, use a Filter to build the condition. This is done using the Define Conditions button. Filters are covered in Chapter 4.

Table 7.1 describes the available actions that you can assign to a Rule, under the "Add Action" button. It also describes the information needed to completely specify the action.

T A B L E   7.1   Actions Assignable to a Rule

ACTION	DESCRIPTION	INFORMATION NEEDED
Send Mail	Generates a new mail message	Complete the mail message dialog box (recipient, subject, message, and so on).
Forward	Forwards a copy of the message	Identify the recipient of the forwarded message, along with a comment.

ACTION	DESCRIPTION	INFORMATION NEEDED
Delegate	Delegates the appointment, reminder, note, or task to another individual	Complete the Delegate dialog box with a recipient comments to both the sender of the original message and the person to whom you are delegating this item.
Reply	Generates a reply to the sender	Specify the recipient (sender or all recipients), whether or not to include the original message, and enter a reply message (subject and message body).
Accept	Accept the appointment, reminder, or note	Select whether to show the accepted item as Free, Busy, Tentative, or Out of the Office, and enter a comment to the sender.
Delete/Decline	Deletes the message or declines the calendar event	Enter a comment for the sender's Sent Items folder.
Empty Item	Purges the item from the Trash Folder	N/A
Move to Folder	Moves the message to a folder	Select the folder and click Move.
Link to Folder	Places a copy of the message in a folder	Select the folder and click Link.
Mark as "Private"	Places a "Private" lock on the item	N/A
Mark as "Read"	Changes the status of the item to "Opened"	N/A
Mark as "Unread"	Changes the status to "Unopened"	N/A
Stop Rule Processing	Ends the processing of a rule	N/A

Using the Proxy Feature

The Proxy feature enables you to access other users' GroupWise messages and Calendars. With this feature you can also permit others to view your GroupWise messages.

Remember, your Mailbox contains all of your GroupWise information: e-mail messages, Calendar items, sent items, deleted messages, personal folders, rules, and so forth. Depending on how your administrator has configured your GroupWise system, your Proxy feature may not apply to all other GroupWise users. Ask your system administrator if your Proxy feature is available to all GroupWise users or limited to users within your post office only.

There are two general steps in setting up a Proxy session:

1. Specify access to a Mailbox — who can access what information, and how (Read? Write? Both?).

2. Start a Proxy session — the process of opening up someone else's Mailbox.

Remember, you cannot access others' Mailboxes until they have given you access privileges to their Mailboxes. Likewise, others cannot access your Mailbox until you have granted them access privileges.

IMPORTANT

Be sure you completely understand the available access privileges before granting them to others. If you are too liberal when granting rights to your Mailbox, other users can send messages that appear to be from you.

Allowing Access to Your Mailbox

You control all access to your Mailbox. Others cannot access your Mailbox unless you first grant them rights. The first thing you need to do is set a password for it (if you haven't already). Next, you need to grant access for any of the three following areas:

- ► Mail and Phone messages

- ► Calendar items (Appointments, Notes, and Tasks)

- ► Notifications, Preferences, and Private Items (Private Items are explained later in this chapter.)

Setting a Password

To provide the highest level of security for your Mailbox, we strongly recommend setting a password. You shouldn't tell anyone your password unless he or she needs to access to your Mailbox.

 NOTE If you use Proxy to access someone else's Mailbox, the password is not required to gain access. The password feature protects against unwanted access by someone to whom you have not granted any access rights.

Setting a password is an option you establish through the Tools menu. (We discuss how to set other options and defaults in Chapter 10.)

To set a password on your Mailbox:

1. Select Tools → Options and double-click the Security icon.

2. Enter a password in the New Password field and in the Confirm New Password field. Choose OK to set the password. The next time you start GroupWise, you will need to type in your password.

 TIP Your password is case-sensitive and is unknown to the administrator or anyone else. If you forget your password, the administrator can remove it or set a new one.

Granting Access to Others

To grant other GroupWise users access rights to your Mailbox:

1. Select Tools → Options and double-click the Security icon.

2. Choose the Proxy Access tab.

3. Click the Address Book button next to the Name: field to start the Address Book. Double-click the user you want to grant access to. Choose OK to add the user to the access list.

 TIP Minimum User Access assigns rights to any GroupWise user that can access your Mailbox. Depending upon the system configuration, this may be any user in the entire GroupWise system. Use caution when making this choice.

4. With the user in the Access List highlighted, select the appropriate access. (See Table 7.2 for a description of the access rights.) Choose OK and Close to apply the rights.

5. To remove a user from the Access List, highlight the user in the Access List and click the Remove User button.

6. To change someone's access, highlight the user in the Access List, change the rights, click OK, and Close to complete the change.

T A B L E   7 . 2   *Proxy Access Fields*

ACCESS RIGHT	DESCRIPTION
Mail/Phone	*Read:* Read messages in your Mailbox folder
	Write: Write e-mail and phone messages in your stead
Appointments	*Read:* Read Posted and Group Appointments from Calendar
	Write: Create Posted Appointments and invite others to meetings in your stead
Reminder Notes	*Read:* Read Personal and Accepted Notes from Calendar
	Write: Create Personal Notes and send Notes in your stead
Tasks	*Read:* Read Posted Tasks and Assigned Tasks from your Calendar or To Do List
	Write: Create Posted Tasks or send Tasks to others in your stead
Subscribe to My Alarms	Enable users to have alarms for your Appointments My Alarms displayed on their computers
Subscribe to My Notifications	Enable users to have notifications for all messages your My Notifications receive displayed on their computers
Modify Options	Enable users to change your preferences (password, Rules/Folders Mailbox access, defaults, and so on), create rules for your Mailbox, and change your folder structure
Archive Items	Enable users to archive any of your messages or Calendar items to their archive files
Read Items	Enable users to read any item (Mail message, Marked Private Appointment, Task, or Note) that is marked Private

You should only grant *Modify options/rules/folders* rights to very trustworthy individuals. These rights enable users to change your password and grant others access to your Mailbox.

NOTE

Starting a Proxy Session

With the Proxy feature, you can access a person's entire Mailbox with the permissions he or she has given you. Having full access to someone else's Mailbox does not mean you can view only the person's messages and Calendar items. You can also access the person's Sent Items, personal folders in the Cabinet, deleted messages in Trash, and the person's rules and preferences. In effect, you become the person who gives you access privileges.

After you are through viewing someone else's Mailbox, you need to start another Proxy session to view your Mailbox again. If you like, you can open an additional GroupWise window for the other user while keeping your Mailbox open. We explain this technique in more detail in the next section.

To start a Proxy session and view someone else's Mailbox:

1. Click the Proxy icon in the lower-left corner of any GroupWise folder, as shown in Figure 7.6. To view someone else's Mailbox, choose the Proxy option from this menu.

2. Type in the username of the user whose Mailbox you want to access, or click the Address Book icon next to the Name: field. Double-click the user from the Address Book and choose OK. You may need to choose the Novell GroupWise Address Book tab to see the list of network users.

3. The Proxy session starts. Note that the last name of the user whose Mailbox you are accessing appears in the GroupWise title bar, as shown in Figure 7.6.

To end the session and view your Mailbox again, click the Proxy icon at the lower-left corner of the main GroupWise screen and click your name on the list. Your Mailbox will open.

Opening Multiple Windows

By default, your main GroupWise window will change to the Mailbox you are accessing with the Proxy feature. This default can be tedious if you need to view multiple Mailboxes; however, you can open a different GroupWise window for each active Proxy session. This multiple-window feature enables you to view many different Mailboxes and Calendars from your workstation.

FIGURE 7.6 *Proxy Session*

Proxy Session Title Bar

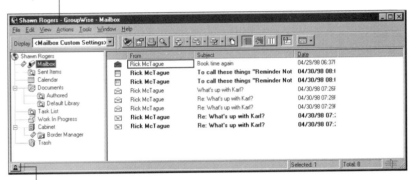

Proxy Icon

TIP

There are other reasons to open multiple GroupWise windows. For example, you can have one window viewing the new messages in your Mailbox, another one showing your open Calendar, and a third window viewing documents in the document library.

To open an extra GroupWise window (with your Mailbox open):

I. Select Window → New Main Window. A new, complete GroupWise window appears on your screen.

2. Click the Proxy icon in the lower-left corner of this new window and start a Proxy session with another Mailbox. This new window displays the Mailbox you are accessing.

3. You can access any of the open windows by choosing that window from the Window menu. Each window is labeled with the last name of the user whose Mailbox is open.

NOTE

As discussed in Chapter 6, you can use the new Multi-User tab in the Calendar Folder View to see multiple user's calendar information on one screen.

Send Options

When you create any type of message — from Mail messages to Tasks — you can specify a number of different *send options* (in other words, options that affect the way GroupWise sends the message). We categorize these options into four categories: general send options, status-tracking options, advanced options, and security options.

To apply one of the send options to a message you are creating:

1. Choose the Properties option under the File menu before you choose Send. The main message option screen appears, as shown in Figure 7.7.

2. The general send options are displayed by default on the Send Options tab. Choose the Status Tracking or Security tab to display those advanced options.

3. Select the desired options, and click OK to apply the options. This message will be sent with the chosen options.

F I G U R E   7.7 *Send Options Screen*

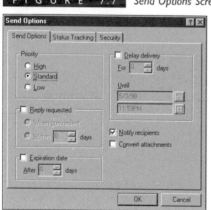

You can set any of these send options as the default. (Setting defaults is covered in Chapter 10.)

General Send, Status Tracking, and Options

Tables 7.3 and 7.4 summarize, respectively, the general send, and status-tracking options. (Asterisks denote default options.)

TABLE 7.3	*General Send Options*	
OPTION	**AVAILABLE CHOICES**	**DESCRIPTION**
Priority	High	Delivered before other messages
	*Standard	Normal Delivery
	Low	Deliver after Standard priority messages
Reply Requested	*Not Selected	No reply requested
	When Convenient	Reply is requested when convenient
	Within *n* days	Reply requested within *n* days (up to 99)
Expiration	*Not Selected	Message deleted from Mailbox by the recipient
	After *n* days	Message deleted from Mailbox after *n* days (up to 250)
Delay Delivery	Delay *n* days	Deliver after *n* days
Delay message delivery for *n* days	Until *date/time*	Delay message delivery until specified *date* and *time*
Notify Recipients	On/Off	Use the Notify program to tell recipients that this message has been delivered
Convert Attachments	On/Off	Convert file attachments that pass through a gateway

TABLE 7.4	Status-Tracking Options	
OPTION	**AVAILABLE CHOICES**	**DESCRIPTION**
Create a sent item to track information	*On/Off	Create an item in your Sent Items folder (or not)
Delivered	On/Off	Status for delivered date and time
*Delivered and Opened	On/Off	Status for delivered and opened
All Information	On/Off	Delivered, opened, deleted, accepted, declined, completed, downloaded, transferred, retracted, replied, and emptied
Auto Delete Sent Item	On/*Off	Delete the message from the sender's Sent Items folder after all recipients have deleted it from their Mailboxes
Return Notification	*None	No notification or Mail (When Opened, Accepted, Completed or Deleted)
	Mail Receipt	New message in Mailbox
	Notify	Notification
	Notify and Mail	Notification and new message in Mailbox

Security Options Tab

The Security Options are divided into two groups: message security options, and mailbox security. Mailbox Security options (such as setting a password) are discussed in Chapter 10. The message security options have to do with the security aspects of messages that you send.

The single default, message security option that comes with GroupWise "out of the box" is "Conceal Subject." The other security options on the Security tab of Send Options enable you to configure the encryption and digital signatures of your messages. These options are only available if you have previously installed an e-mail encryption program that is "GroupWise enabled."

Entrust Technologies, Inc. is one company who has created security solutions for desktop computing applications, such as GroupWise. If the Entrust security software is installed on your computer, the additional options on the Security tab of Send Options will be available. If not, they will be grayed out. More information on Entrust Technologies is available at: www.entrust.com.

Mark Private

Sometimes you want to put information in your Calendar that is so private you don't want even your closest proxy associates to see it. You just want them to know you are busy. An extra measure of control on any item in your Mailbox — e-mail messages, appointments, tasks, notes, or any other message — is marking the item Private. Marking the item private does not change the way GroupWise handles the message, but it does place a lock on the item.

You want to mark items private when you have granted others access to your Mailbox. Unless you grant them the right called Read Items Marked Private, any item you mark as private will be invisible to them.

To mark an item private, simply highlight the item and choose Actions → Mark Private, or press F8.

NOTE If the item being marked as private is a Calendar item, a padlock icon appears next to the item. If it is any other kind of item, no indication is given that the item is private, except for a check mark next to the Mark Private option under the Actions menu.

To remove the Private setting, highlight the item and choose the Mark Private option under the Actions menu. This action removes the check mark.

Discussions (Posted Messages)

In GroupWise terminology, a *discussion* is an advanced message type that enables related messages to appear under one umbrella, called a *Discussion Area*. These messages are posted in the discussion area's Shared Folder. You can view the history of people's thought processes and the flow of their posted messages in a Discussion Area by using the Discussion Thread option under the View menu.

The terms *Discussion, Discussion Area,* and *Posted Message* are synonymous.

NOTE

Discussion Areas and Posted Message are created, stored, and accessed through Shared Folders. For more information about Shared Folders, see Chapter 4.

It is a good idea to include the word "discussion" in the name of the Shared Folder that will hold discussions to differentiate it from other Shared Folders.

TIP

To create a new Discussion:

I. Highlight a shared folder in the Folders Area.

2. Choose File → New. Select Discussion from the list of message types.

As a short cut, you can click the down arrow next to the Create New Mail button on the Toolbar and choose Posted Message.

TIP

3. Enter a subject line and message body, and attach any files you wish by clicking the paper clip at the bottom of the New Discussion screen, as shown in Figure 7.8. This box will be labeled "New Posted Message" if you used the Toolbar method.

4. Click Post to place the new discussion in the shared folder.

F I G U R E   7 . 8   *A New Discussion Screen*

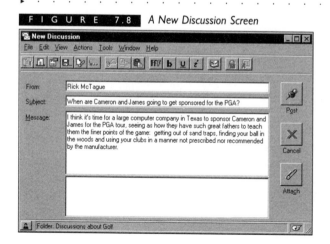

TIP

The Posted Discussion and all replies will have a thumbtack and piece of paper symbol next to them, which is the icon for a discussion message.

To read and reply to a discussion message:

1. Highlight a shared folder in the Folders Area.

2. Choose View → Display Settings → Discussion Thread. The discussions in this folder will appear, along with the replies in a nested fashion.

3. Double-click the discussion or reply you wish to read.

4. To create a reply, click Reply. You'll see the dialog box shown in Figure 7.9.

IMPORTANT

If someone is currently creating a reply to a discussion message, no one else can read the discussion message until the reply is complete.

F I G U R E 7.9   *Replying to a Discussion*

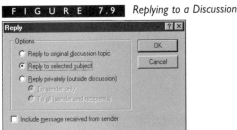

If you would like to post a reply in the Discussion Area, choose either the Reply to selected subject options or the Reply to original discussion topic option in the Reply dialog box. Your reply will appear under the appropriate message.

If you wish to reply to any part of a discussion and not include your reply in the shared folder, select Reply privately (outside discussion). Then send your reply as a regular mail message to the sender only or to all participants in the discussion.

Discussions are useful for quickly sharing information with a large group of people and for achieving smooth work flow. Discussions also provide a public, recorded history of communications at your organization.

Message Threads

When you have a Shared Folder full of discussions and replies, you need a quick and easy way to navigate through that information.

The first task is to view the messages as discussions. This is done by clicking the Shared Folder that holds Discussions and choosing View → Display Settings → Discussion Threads. To scan through the posted discussions and their replies easily, click the first message in the discussion (it will be left-justified on the screen and have a plus sign (+) next to it. Then choose View → Threads. You will see a menu choice as displayed in Figure 7.10. The Next option highlights the next item in the discussion, and Previous highlights the previous one. The Expand and Collapse options expand and collapse the listing of discussions and their replies.

F I G U R E 7.10 *Navigating Discussions Using Message Threads*

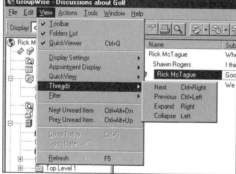

Appearance Options

As you are typing a message, you may decide you want to change the appearance of the text. You can change the appearance by choosing from the various appearance options. You can enlarge the font (type size), change the color, or make characters bold or italic.

To change the appearance of the message you are creating:

1. Select the text to be formatted by clicking the first character of the first word and holding down the mouse button while dragging it to the end of the last word. Release the mouse button, and notice that the selected text is highlighted. (Alternatively, hold down the Shift key and use the arrow keys to move the cursor and highlight the text.)

2. Choose Edit → Font, which opens a small submenu. To make the text bold, italic, underlined, or normal (remove formatting), click your selection from this menu. (Alternatively, press Ctrl+B to bold the text, Ctrl+U to underline the text, or Ctrl+I to italicize the text; or, use the formatting buttons on the Toolbar.)

3. To change the font, font size, or font color, choose Font from the submenu, and complete the dialog box shown in Figure 7.11. Choose OK to apply the changes.

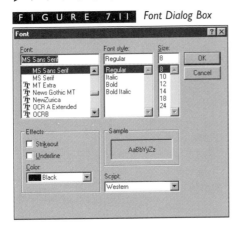

FIGURE 7.11 *Font Dialog Box*

OLE Attachments

GroupWise 5's compatibility with industry standards, such as Object Linking and Embedding (OLE), makes it easy to share information among applications.

OLE is used to make an active bridge between different types of data (spreadsheet, database, document, and so on). This bridge is used to update all associated data types when one of them changes.

An extensive discussion of OLE is beyond the scope of this book, but we do want to show you how to add these objects to a GroupWise message. There are five operations you can use to add OLE objects to your messages:

> ➤ File, Attachments, Attach Object — Add an OLE object as a file attachment. Select the object and choose OK, as shown in Figure 7.12.

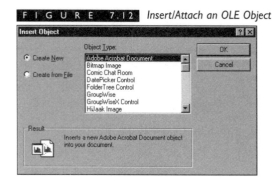

FIGURE 7.12 *Insert/Attach an OLE Object*

To embed a Word document into a GroupWise attachment (so the recipient can double-click the attachment to open the application, instead of just viewing the file):

1. From a new message screen, choose File → Attachments → Attach Object.

2. Make sure that Create New is selected and choose Microsoft Word Document from the list of object types. Click OK.

3. Microsoft Word launches, and the new, open document is created as an attachment to the GroupWise message.

4. Make the necessary additions to the document and choose File → Close and Return to GroupWise to attach the new document.

5. From the new GroupWise message window, click the Send button to send the document out.

6. The recipient opens the message as normal and launches Microsoft Word with the file you created.

Date Difference

The Date Difference utility may seem like a fluffy feature on the surface, one that is hardly worth mentioning. However, if you need to know exactly how many calendar days there are between a certain range of dates, this utility comes in handy.

Obviously, the value of this utility comes in when calculating the date difference across months and years.

To start the Date Difference utility, click Tools → Date Difference.

To calculate the number of days between a range of dates, click the Start date in the left-hand side of the dialog box show in Figure 7.13.

F I G U R E   7 . 1 3 *Date Difference Dialog Box*

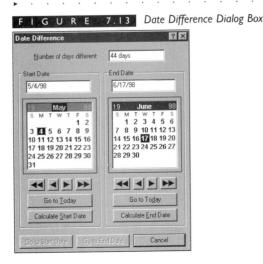

Click the End date in the right-hand side of the dialog box. You will see the number of days within this range at the top of the screen, in the Number of days different box.

You can also enter a desired number of days in the Number of days different box at the top, click a desired start date and click the Calculate End Date button to see the calculated end date.

The opposite is true, also. You can enter a desired number of days in the Number of days different box, click the desired End date and click the Calculate Start Date button on the left-hand side of the dialog box to see the calculated Start date.

This utility is very useful for creating fixed-length tasks.

TIP

Summary

In this chapter, you saw how the powerful advanced features in GroupWise can help you be more productive. Mastering sending options, rules, discussions, and the other advanced topics we covered will set you apart as a true GroupWise guru.

CHAPTER 8

Document Management

Document management is very different from file management. In file management, you store your files in directories and subdirectories on your hard drive (or on a network drive). In document management, all documents are stored in a central location on a network. Instead of storing your files in directories and subdirectories, your documents are stored in a database system.

The document management capabilities built into GroupWise 5 make it a unique product in the e-mail and groupware industry. GroupWise document management services is a feature that enables you to manage your documents in your GroupWise system. By integrating messaging and document management, GroupWise makes it easy to access and share documents with others.

You can use GroupWise document management features to:

▸ Store document files in the GroupWise system

▸ Access common files shared by members of your organization, company, or department and share your files with other users

▸ Maintain multiple versions of documents

▸ Search for documents stored in the system

NOTE

GroupWise Document Management must be configured at the GroupWise system level before individual users can utilize document management features. If you are unsure about whether document management is available at your organization, ask your system administrator. By default, document management is configured automatically in GroupWise 5.5.

Document Libraries

Document libraries are the heart of GroupWise document management systems. A library is a document storage location in a GroupWise system. Each library is set up by the system administrator. GroupWise users store documents in libraries and access shared documents that are stored there.

A GroupWise library is similar to a real-world public library. If you need a particular book, you can quickly find out if it is at the library by checking the card catalog system. You can locate a particular book by its author, title, or subject matter. Instead of books, GroupWise libraries store documents. You can find a document in a GroupWise library by running a search based on its title, author, or subject, as well as a number of other criteria collectively known as *document properties*.

Accessing Libraries

The system administrator sets up each library and determines library access privileges. For example, the administrator may set up a library that contains documents that everyone in the company needs to access, such as product marketing documents and expense report forms. The administrator may decide to grant View rights only so everyone can read the documents, but nobody except the administrator can change them. If your personal documents will be stored in the library, the administrator will need to grant you different access rights for those documents. To manage your personal documents in a library, you need to be able to view, create, modify, and delete them.

If you have questions about what you can or cannot do within a library in your system, ask your administrator. By default, you should have access to at least one library with rights to store documents in that library.

Using Library Documents

Once a document is placed into a library, it can only be accessed through GroupWise or through an application that uses GroupWise document management services (called an integrated application).

Many Windows 95 applications support GroupWise document management, such as the latest versions of Microsoft Word, Microsoft Excel, WordPerfect, and Quattro Pro.

If you need to work on a document when you are not logged into GroupWise, you must first "check out" the document from the library and place it in a directory or on a disk. When you are finished working on the document, you check it back into the library. We explain how to check out and check in documents later in this chapter.

Documents stored in the library can be accessed in two ways: through document references in your GroupWise Mailboxes or through document searches. A document reference is an icon in your Mailbox, similar to a Mail message icon. Both methods are explained later in this chapter.

Setting a Default Library

A default library is the library where you store your documents by default. Although you may have access to many GroupWise libraries, you should specify one library as your default library. If you are running GroupWise 5.5 or later, you should already have a default library configured unless the default configuration was modified by your administrator.

To set a default library:

1. Select Tools → Options.

2. Double-click the Documents icon. The dialog box shown in Figure 8.1 appears.

3. Highlight the library you want as your default library, and click the Set Default button.

4. Click OK to save your settings, then click Close to exit Options.

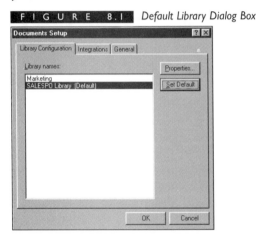

FIGURE 8.1 *Default Library Dialog Box*

IMPORTANT

All libraries to which you have been granted the View right will appear in the list when you double-click the Documents icon. However, if you plan to store personal documents in your default library, you will need more than just the View right. Your system administrator can tell you which libraries are suitable for storing personal documents.

After you designate a default library, you can perform all of the document management functions that are enabled by your rights assignments. Of course, before you can do anything with library documents, the documents must first be placed in the library. You place documents in a library by either importing them or by creating them in the library.

Importing Documents into a Library

There are two methods for importing documents into a library: Quick Import and Custom Import.

IMPORTANT

Once a document is moved into a library, it can only be accessed through GroupWise or applications that integrate with GroupWise document management services. For example, if you create a document using Microsoft Word and save it in the library, you can still work on the document, but you must use the GroupWise document management dialog boxes to retrieve the document in Word. You can choose to copy documents into the library and maintain a copy outside of the library, but you must then decide how both versions will be kept current.

Using Quick Import

Quick Import copies your documents into the default library with the default document property settings. (Document properties are explained later in this chapter.) Quick Import does not let you customize documents individually. Use a Quick Import when you need to place many files into the library all at once and you are not concerned about customizing the document properties for each document.

To perform a Quick Import:

1. Select File → Import Documents. The dialog box shown in Figure 8.2 appears. Notice that the Quick Import option is selected by default.

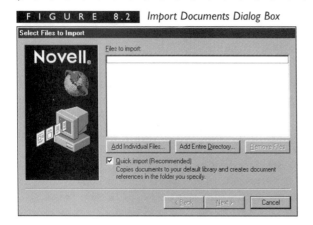

FIGURE 8.2 *Import Documents Dialog Box*

2. Click either the Add Individual Files button or the Add Entire Directory button.

3. If you selected the Add Individual Files option, navigate to the desired directory, highlight the files you want to import, and click OK. Repeat this step to add files from other directories.

4. If you selected the Add Entire Directory button, navigate to the desired directory or directories and place check marks in the boxes next to the directories that contain files you want to import.

5. Repeat Steps 2, 3, and 4 until all the files and directories are listed in the Import dialog box.

6. Click Next when all files are listed in the Import dialog box. The Create Document References dialog box appears, as shown in Figure 8.3.

7. Choose the Import without displaying documents in a folder option to import the documents into the library without creating document references in your Mailbox, or choose the Display documents in a folder option to create document references in a folder you specify.

8. If you chose to display the documents in a folder, click a check box in the Select Folder window to designate where the document references will appear. (Note: If you don't select a folder, a document reference will not be created.)

FIGURE 8.3 *Create Document References Dialog Box*

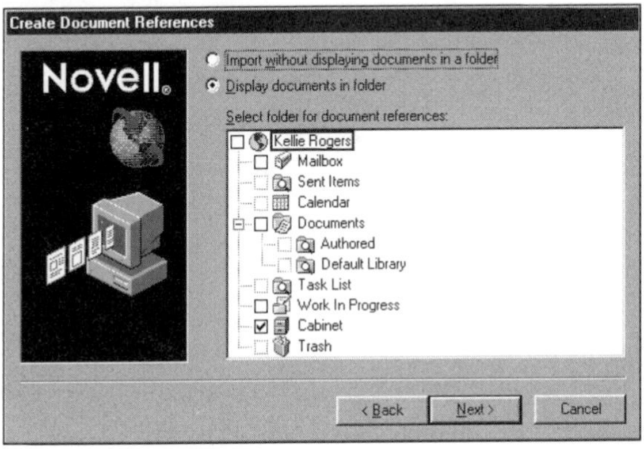

Create Document References

Novell.

○ Import without displaying documents in a folder
◉ Display documents in folder

Select folder for document references:

☐ 🌐 Kellie Rogers
├─ ☐ 📬 Mailbox
├─ ☐ 📧 Sent Items
├─ ☐ 📅 Calendar
├─ ☐ 📁 Documents
│ ├─ 📁 Authored
│ └─ 📁 Default Library
├─ ☐ 📋 Task List
├─ ☐ 📁 Work In Progress
├─ ☑ 📁 Cabinet
└─ ☐ 🗑 Trash

[< Back] [Next >] [Cancel]

9. Click Next.

10. Click Finish to perform the import or Back to modify your selected options. An import progress dialog box will appear, showing you the status of the import, and if any of the documents have failed to import correctly.

IMPORTANT

Quick Import copies documents into the library and leaves the files in your directory structure unchanged.

Using Custom Import

Custom Import gives you much more control over importing documents into the library. Custom Import enables you to:

▸ Specify which library you will import the documents into

▸ Specify document properties on a per-document basis

▸ Move or Copy documents into the library

To import documents using Custom Import:

1. Select File → Import Documents.

2. Clear the Quick Import option by clicking the check box.

3. Click either the Add Individual Files button or the Add Entire Directory button.

4. If you selected the Add Individual Files option, navigate to the desired directory, highlight the files you want to import, and click OK. Repeat this step to add files from other directories. If you selected the Add Entire Directory button, navigate to the desired directory or directories and place check marks in the boxes next to the directories that contain files you want to import.

5. Repeat Steps 2, 3, and 4 until all the files and directories are listed in the Import dialog box.

6. Click Next when all files are listed in the Import dialog box.

7. Click Next. The Import Method dialog box appears.

8. Choose between the Copy files into GroupWise and the Move files into GroupWise options and click Next.

IMPORTANT

The Move option removes the files from your directories and places them in the library. Be sure you don't accidentally move operating system or application files into the library.

9. (Optional) If you want a log file, select the Store all status and error messages into a log file option, and specify a path and filename for the log file.

10. Click Next. The Select Library dialog box appears.

11. Select the library into which the files will be imported, and click Next. The Create Document References dialog box appears.

12. Choose the Import Without Displaying Documents in a Folder option to import the documents into the library without creating document references in your Mailbox. Or choose the Display documents in a folder option to create document references in a folder you specify.

13. If you chose to display the documents in a folder, click a check box in the Select Folder window to designate where the document references appear. Click Next. The Set Document Property Options dialog box appears, as shown in Figure 8.4.

14. Choose the Prompt for properties of each document individually option if you want to set different document properties for each document you chose in Steps 4 and 5. (This could be time-consuming if you are importing many documents.) Alternatively, choose the Set properties using default values option to use the default properties for all documents.

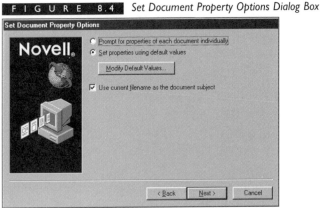

FIGURE 8.4 *Set Document Property Options Dialog Box*

15. (Optional) Use the Modify Default Values button to establish default document properties for the files being imported.

16. If you don't want the document filename to be the document subject line for each document, clear the Use current filename as the document subject check box. (If you clear the check box, you are prompted to enter a subject for each document individually. Again, this could be tedious if you are importing many documents.)

17. Click Next. The Import Document dialog box appears.

18. Click Finish to start the import process or Back to modify your selections.

After the import finishes, document references will appear in the folder you selected (if you chose the Create Reference option) and your documents will be available from the library. Remember, these documents cannot be accessed by others because you have not set up sharing properties. Also, remember that you must be running GroupWise to access the documents in the library.

Creating New Documents

In addition to importing existing documents into a GroupWise library, you can create new documents in a library.

To create a new document:

1. From the main GroupWise screen, select File → New.

2. Click Document. The New Document dialog box appears, as shown in Figure 8.5. When you create a new document, GroupWise prompts you to select a method for creating the document. You can select an application, a template, or a file. These options are explained in Table 8.1.

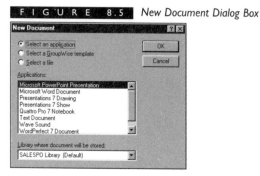

FIGURE 8.5 *New Document Dialog Box*

3. If you want to use a specific application to create the document, select the application and click OK. If you want to base the document on a template, select the template and click OK. If, instead, you want to base the document on a file, select the file and click OK. The New Document dialog box appears, prompting you to enter a subject for the document.

4. Enter a subject.

5. If you want to open the document, verify that the Open Document Now check box is selected, and click OK. GroupWise will open the application that is associated with the document type, the application, or the file extension, depending upon the creation method you selected. For example, if the file extension is .DOC, GroupWise will launch Microsoft Word.

TIP

WiseGuide: If you are opening an application that does not support GroupWise document management, you will get a warning stating that you are opening a nonintegrated application. Click OK to bypass the warning. If you don't want to see the warning again, click the "Don't show this message again" check box. You can use nonintegrated applications with GroupWise document management; just don't change the filename that is assigned by GroupWise when the document is open.

6. Create the document using the application.

7. Save the document using the assigned filename.

8. Close the application.

The document will be saved in the GroupWise library.

TABLE 8.1	Options for Creating a New Document
OPTION	**FUNCTION**
Select an Application	You can select an application to create a document based on that application. The Applications list box shows all the applications that are registered in the Windows registry.
Select a GroupWise Template	A template is a file you use to create other documents, such as a word processing document preformatted with the company letterhead, or a spreadsheet file that is set up to calculate an expense report.
	You can select GroupWise templates to use a document in the library as the foundation of a new document.
	If you have documents that you often use as a basis for creating new documents, you can add them to the library and assign them the template document type. These templates will then appear in the templates list.
Select a File	You can select a file anywhere on your system and use it as a foundation for a new document.

Creating Document References

When you create or import a document into the library, you have the option to create a document reference within a GroupWise folder. A document reference is similar to the icons you see in the Mailbox when you receive a Mail message. It is a pointer you use to access the document in the library.

TIP

WiseGuide: If a document already exists in the library and you just want to create a document reference for it in your Mailbox, click File → New → Document Reference. You can also create a document reference by using the GroupWise Find feature to locate a document and drag the document to your Mailbox or other folder.

Figure 8.6 shows a Mailbox that contains several document references. Notice that the icons resemble the applications that created the documents.

FIGURE 8.6 Document References in the Mailbox

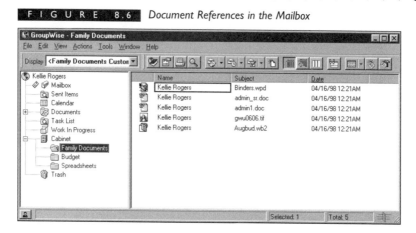

A document reference can exist in the same folders as GroupWise Mail messages, or you can create folders in your Mailbox for your documents (just like you would create directories in a file system).

Checking Out Documents

When you open a document from the library, the document is marked as In Use and cannot be opened and modified by other users. However, there may be times when you want to work on the document while you are not running GroupWise. For example, you may need to modify the document while at home or while on a business trip. In this situation, you would need to "check out" the document.

When you check out a document, the document is marked as In Use until you check it back in. The document cannot be modified by other users; however, the document can be viewed by GroupWise users who have View rights. You have two options when checking out documents:

▸ Check Out Only

▸ Check Out and Copy

If you choose the Check Out Only option, the document is marked as Checked out in the library and cannot be modified by others, but it is not copied to a directory for you to access it.

If you choose the Check Out and Copy option, the document is copied to the directory you specify.

WiseGuide: To find out who has a document checked out of the library, right-click the document reference and choose Properties. Select the Activity Log tab.

TIP

To check out a document:

1. Highlight the document reference in your Mailbox.

2. Click Actions → Check-Out. The dialog box shown in Figure 8.7 appears.

3. Type a filename for the document in the Checked-Out Filename field. (By default, GroupWise uses the document number as the check-out filename. You can specify a different filename.)

4. Enter a path for the document in the Checked-Out Location field.

5. Click the Check-Out button.

Once you have checked out a document, you can open it from the directory and change it while you are not running GroupWise. The changes you make do not appear in the document in the library until you check it back in or update it.

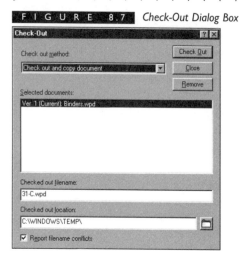

FIGURE 8.7 *Check-Out Dialog Box*

Checking in Documents

After you are finished with a document that you have checked out from a library, you must check the document back in so any changes are reflected in the library. Checking in a document unlocks the document so it can be modified by other users.

TIP

You can check in multiple documents at once by holding Ctrl and clicking multiple documents in the Documents to be Checked In dialog box.

To check in a document:

1. Highlight the document reference in your Mailbox.
2. Click Actions and then Check-In. The dialog box shown in Figure 8.8 appears.
3. Choose the Check-in method.

Check-In Dialog Box

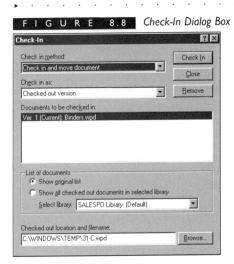

You have four options for checking in documents, as shown in Table 8.2. When you check in a document, you also have three options that relate to document versions, as shown in Table 8.3.

T A B L E   8 . 2   *Check-In Method Options*

OPTION	EXPLANATION
Check In and Move	Moves the document to the library and deletes it from the check-out location
Check In and Copy	Copies the document to the library and leaves a copy in the check-out location
Check In Only	Checks the document back in to the library, but does not update the document in the library with any changes you made to the checked-out version
Update Without Checking In	Updates the document in the library with the changes you have made, but does not unlock the document

TABLE 8.3	*Check-In Version Options*
OPTION	**EXPLANATION**
Checked-out version	Keeps the same document version as the version you checked out
New version	Enables you to specify a new document version
New Document	Enables you to create an entirely new document in the library and specify new document properties

Remember that if you are updating documents and you are connected to the GroupWise system, you do not have to go through the check-out, check-in process. When you open a document in the library, it is marked as In Use until you close the document. Other users cannot open and modify the document while you have it open. You only need to check out a document when you will be working on it while not connected to GroupWise.

Copying Documents

Use the document copy feature to create a document identical to one in the library and make changes without altering the original.

When you copy a document, you need to specify the new document's properties. You can manually specify the properties, or you can use the properties of the source document.

To copy a document:

1. Highlight one or more document references in your Mailbox.

2. Select Actions → Copy Document. The Copy Document dialog box appears, as shown in Figure 8.9.

3. Choose the library where the document will be copied to from the drop-down list.

4. Specify the method for creating the properties for the new document(s).

5. Click OK.

New document references appear in your Mailbox.

FIGURE 8.9 *Copy Document Dialog Box*

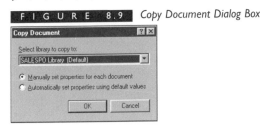

Deleting Documents

If you have Delete rights, you can delete documents from the library. You have three choices when deleting documents:

- ▸ **Delete the document reference from your Mailbox.** Only the document reference is removed and the document itself remains in the library.

- ▸ **Delete the selected version of the document.** The document reference is removed from your Mailbox and previous versions remain in the library.

- ▸ **Delete all versions of the document.** The document reference is removed from your Mailbox and all versions of the document are removed from the library.

GroupWise automatically deletes documents that have exceeded their defined document life, as specified in the document type definition. Each document type has an expiration date and expiration action (delete or archive).

To delete a document:

1. Highlight the document reference in your Mailbox.

2. Select Edit → Delete. The dialog box shown in Figure 8.10 appears.

3. Choose the deletion method you want.

4. Click OK.

FIGURE 8.10 *Delete Dialog Box*

Document Searches

One of the advantages of document management is that it makes finding documents easy. Instead of hunting through directories and trying to recognize cryptic eight-character filenames, with GroupWise document management, you can search for documents using a number of different criteria.

Document Properties

Each document in a GroupWise library has a set of attributes that uniquely identifies the document, such as the author's name, the date the document was created, and the document type. These attributes are *document properties*. You use document properties to find documents that have been placed in a library.

You can set document properties when you import a document into the library or when you create the document. You can also edit the document properties through the document reference, by right-clicking on the reference and selecting the Properties option. The document properties dialog box is shown in Figure 8.11.

F I G U R E   8.11 *Document Properties Dialog Box*

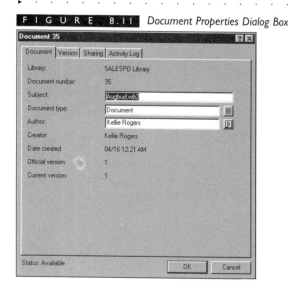

As shown in Figure 8.11, there are four categories of document properties: Document, Version, Sharing, and Activity Log. The most common document properties and their descriptions are listed in Table 8.4.

T A B L E 8 . 4	Document Properties
PROPERTY	**DESCRIPTION**
Library	The library that contains the document.
Document Number	A number assigned by GroupWise that is used by the document management system to identify the document.
Subject	A text field that enables you to assign a descriptive subject for the document, such as "1996 Annual Report."
	When you import documents, you have the option to make the filename and path the document subject. Otherwise, you can specify the subject as you create the document, or you can edit the subject in the properties dialog box.
Document Type	A classification for the document that is used to categorize and establish the usage of the document. For example, some common document types include: Agenda, Contract, Memo, Minutes, Proposal, and Report.
	These classifications, or types, facilitate searches for specific documents. An important field in Document Type is the expiration setting. The expiration setting determines when a document expires and what should be done with the document when it expires.
Author	The author of the document. The author is not always the same as the creator. The author can be any GroupWise user.
Creator	The person who placed the document in the library.

(continued)

TABLE 8.4 *(continued)*

PROPERTY	DESCRIPTION
Date Created	The date and time the document was placed in the library. (Note: If you imported the document from a file system, the date and time stamp on the file is not preserved in the document properties.)
Current Version	GroupWise document management services allow up to 100 versions of a document. The current version is the latest version of the document.
Official Version	The version of the document that will be identified and viewed through searches. For example, if seven versions of the annual report were stored in the library, and version 6 was designated as the official version, it would be the version found in searches by GroupWise users who have View rights to the library. (Version 7 could be a draft in progress that is not yet ready for official release.)
	Any version of a document can be identified as the official version. If you do not specify an official version, the current version is the official version. Usually the official version is designated by the creator of the document, but the right to set the official version can be granted to others.
Description	A text field that enables you to describe the current version of the document. By default, the description for the first version of a document will be "Original."
Status	The document status possibilities include:
	Available. The document is available to be opened or checked out of the library.
	In Use. Another user currently has the document opened or checked out.
	Checked-Out. Another user has checked out the document.
Sharing	Shows the GroupWise users with whom you have shared the documents. You control the sharing properties for the documents you add to the library. By default, a document is not shared and cannot be accessed by other users. Sharing documents is discussed later in this chapter. (Note: The rights you specify for shared documents apply to all versions of the document.)

PROPERTY	DESCRIPTION
Activity Log	The Activity Log property shows you a chronological log of the actions that have been performed on the document, such as who created the document, who has opened the document, who has viewed the document, and who has edited the document.

IMPORTANT

You must have the Edit right to the library to change a document's properties. You likely have this right for your documents, but you may not have this right for public documents.

Setting Default Document Properties

You can set default properties that will be used for all documents you import or create. To set default document properties:

1. Select Tools → Options.

2. Double-click the Documents icon.

3. Click the Properties tab.

4. In the Property configuration screen, select the document property fields that you want available for your documents by default.

5. In the Document Defaults tab, you can specify a default document subject, document type, and author.

6. In the Sharing tab, you can set default sharing options. This is useful if you want all of the documents you add to the library shared with others by default.

7. Choose OK when finished setting default document properties.

The values you set become the default properties for any documents you create or import in the library.

Using Find

In Chapter 4, we discuss how to use the Find feature. The Advanced Find options are very useful for searching document libraries.

NOTE

When you use the Find feature, GroupWise searches for your document in the default library first.

To find a document using Standard Find options:

1. Select Tools → Find.

2. Specify a full text search or a subject line search.

3. Type the word or words you want to find in the text box.

4. (Optional) Specify the item type you want to search for, such as e-mail or document.

5. (Optional) Specify the item source, such as received or posted.

6. (Optional) Specify a date range to search.

7. Specify the folders to search by clicking the boxes next to the folders.

8. Click OK to perform the search.

You can expand the Mailbox to select individual folders or the All Libraries icon to select individual libraries.

TIP

GroupWise will perform the search and return a list of documents or messages that meet your specified search criteria.

To find a document using Advanced Find options:

1. Select Tools → Find.

2. Click the Advanced Find button.

3. Specify the find criteria using the Advanced Find dialog box. Figure 8.12 shows how to find all entries where the author is Kellie Rogers, the library is the SalesPO Library, and the subject contains the word *golf*.

4. Click OK to accept the advanced search criteria.

5. Specify any additional search options and click OK to begin the search.

GroupWise presents you with a list of the documents that met the search criteria.

F I G U R E   8.12   *Advanced Find*

Advanced Find	? X

Filter

Include entries where ... Author is 'Kellie Rogers' and Library is 'SALESPO Library' and Subject contains 'golf'

Author	=	Kellie Rogers	And
Library	=	SALESPO Library	And
Subject	[]	golf	End

OK
Cancel
Clear

Document Sharing

When you place documents in a library, you control who has access to those documents through the Sharing tab of the document properties screen. You also control what rights others have to the document.

To share a document with other users:

1. Right-click the document reference in your Mailbox and choose Properties.

2. Click the Sharing tab. The dialog box shown in Figure 8.13 appears. The default sharing property is Not Shared. Not Shared means that no other GroupWise user has access to the document. Notice that GroupWise inserts General User Access and Creator Access in the Share list. By default, general users (all users with access to the library) do not have any rights to the document and the author/creator has full rights to the document.

3. Click the Shared With option.

4. Type the user name in the Name: field and click Add User. Alternatively, you can click the Address Book tab and double-click the user's name in the address list. The user name appears in the Share List window.

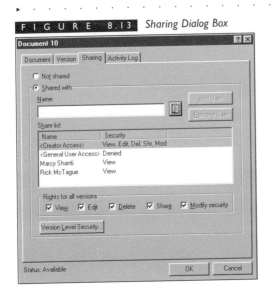

By default, the new users have the View right, which means that the users can locate the document in searches and can view the document, but cannot modify it.

IMPORTANT The rights you specify are for all versions of a document. If you want to specify different rights for each version of a document, click the Version Level Security button.

To specify additional rights:

1. Highlight the user in the Share List window.

2. Click the check boxes for Edit, Delete, Share, or Modify Security to grant those rights. Table 8.5 lists the user rights options for a document.

T A B L E 8 . 5	User Rights Options for a Document
RIGHT	**DESCRIPTION**
Edit	Users can make changes to the document.
Delete	Users can delete the document. Use this right with care.
Share	Users can add the document to shared folders, thereby sharing the document with other GroupWise users.
Modify Security	Users can modify the rights for the document. If you grant this right, the users can modify the other rights, and could grant themselves the Edit and Delete rights.

Use the General User Access entry to grant the same rights to all users who have access to the library. For example, if for some reason you want everyone to be able to delete the file, highlight General User Access and grant the Delete right.

NOTE A user must have the Edit right before he or she can have the Modify Security right.

When you grant users Edit or Delete rights, GroupWise automatically gives them View rights to the document. Without the View right, a user cannot see the document in the results of a Find, in shared folders, and so on.

When you grant other users rights to the document, the users do not automatically receive a document reference in their Mailboxes. They can only access the document by using Find.

Using Query Folders with Document Management

The query folder feature of GroupWise is very powerful when combined with the GroupWise document management capabilities. You can create query folders that allow you to display only documents that have specific properties.

A common use of query folders is to display the document references of all the documents you have stored in the library, or to create folders that contain the document references of specific document types, such as contracts.

To create a query folder that displays all of your documents:

1. Right-click a folder and select New Folder.
2. Select the Find Results folder type.
3. Select the Custom Find Results Folder.
4. Click Next.
5. Give the folder a name.
6. (Optional) Give the folder a description.
7. Click Next.
8. In the Create Find Results dialog box, select only Documents as the Item Type.
9. (Optional) Change the View by, Sort by, and Sort order so the items display according to your personal preference.
10. Click Next.
11. In the Create Find Results Folder dialog box, enter your name in the From/Author field.
12. Select Document as the Item Type.
13. Specify which Libraries should be searched by the query folder.
14. (Optional) Set any other options you desire, such as a date range.
15. Click Finish.

This folder will now display all of the library documents that you have authored.

Performing Mass Document Operations

GroupWise document management services allow you to perform operations on many documents at once by using the Mass Document Operations option. With this option, you can perform these operations on several documents at once:

- ► Change document properties
- ► Move
- ► Delete
- ► Change sharing
- ► Copy

For example, if you need to move or copy a large number of documents from one GroupWise library to another, you should use the Mass Document Operations option.

To use the Mass Document Operations option:

1. (Optional) In your GroupWise mailbox, highlight the documents on which you want to perform the operation.

2. Select Tools → Mass Document Operations. The dialog box in Figure 8.14 appears.

F I G U R E ' 8.14 *Mass Document Operations Dialog Box*

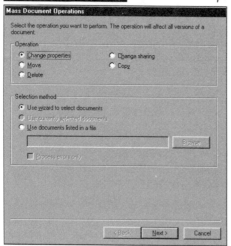

3. Select the desired operation: Move, Change Properties, Delete, Change Sharing, or Copy.

4. Choose your selection method: Wizard, Documents Listed in File, or Currently Selected documents. The Wizard takes you through a series of dialog boxes that helps you locate the documents.

5. Click Next.

Follow the prompts to perform the operation.

► . . . . ◄

Echoing Documents to Your Remote Mailbox

If you use the remote features of GroupWise (discussed in the next chapter), you can "echo" documents from your default library to a library created in your remote mailbox, which is located on your hard drive.

This feature lets you work on documents that are stored in the library locally while you are not connected to your master GroupWise mailbox. This feature maintains two copies of your documents, one in the library and one in your GroupWise remote mailbox stored on your local hard drive.

When you reconnect, you can then update the documents you have modified. To enable document echoing:

1. Select Tools → Options.

2. Double-click the Documents Icon.

3. Select the General tab.

4. Choose the Echo Documents to GroupWise Remote option.

5. Click OK.

Documents will be echoed to your remote mailbox whenever you close or check in a document in your master mailbox. A document reference is created for the echoed document in your remote mailbox.

► . . . . ◄

Summary

In this chapter we explain the basics of document management. The Group-Wise online help system provides extensive information about document management and also includes a guide entitled "Managing Your Documents" to help you get started.

In the next chapter we explain how to use GroupWise Remote Mode to remain connected while you are away from the office.

CHAPTER 9

Remote Mode

With today's mobile workforce, access to e-mail and scheduling information is more critical than ever. If you can access your messaging system regardless of where you are, you can communicate with your customers and coworkers as if you were sitting in your office.

This chapter addresses how to configure the GroupWise client for remote access. We look at the steps necessary to access information when you're out of the office — how to request your messages and how to connect to the system and download your messages. We also explain the different techniques to use when you are connected to a network and when you are working off-line using a remote Mailbox.

Preparing to Use GroupWise in Remote Mode

Before we get into the actual mouse clicks and keystrokes needed to configure and use GroupWise in Remote Mode, there is some information gathering that you need to do. Your GroupWise system administrator needs to provide you with some information that GroupWise will ask you for: domain name, post office name, phone number of the Async gateway, login ID, and password.

You also need to find out how you are going to connect to the GroupWise system when you are not in the office. There are three types of connections possible:

- ▶ **Network:** Using a drive letter and path to your post office on a network, possibly achieved through a dial-in, network-connection software package such as NetWare Connect.

- ▶ **TCP/IP:** Using the TCP/IP address of the GroupWise Mail server that synchronizes your Master Mailbox with your Remote Mailbox.

- ▶ **Modem:** Using a dial-up connection to the GroupWise Async gateway that forwards your incoming and outgoing messages.

The next step in preparing to set up GroupWise Remote Mode is assigning a password to your Master Mailbox. You need to set a password on your Master Mailbox before GroupWise 5 Remote Mode will work. You must do this while you are logged into the network.

To set a password on your Master Mailbox:

I. Select Tools → Options and double-click the Security icon.

2. Type a password in the New Password field and in the Confirm New Password field. Click OK to set the password. The next time you start GroupWise, you will need to type in your password. (If you never log into the network, the system administrator can set a password on your Mailbox and tell you what it is.)

IMPORTANT

The password is case-sensitive. Also, be sure to record your password somewhere secure.

Finally, you need to install GroupWise 5 on the hard drive of the computer you will be using in Remote Mode. You should contact your system administrator to help you set this up. (If the computer you use at work is the same as the computer you use when working off-line in Remote Mode, simply make sure GroupWise is installed on the hard drive. The standard GroupWise client is all you need to run in Remote Mode.)

Configuring the GroupWise Client

If you start the GroupWise program while you are not connected to or logged into the network, choose Path to Remote Mailbox from the dialog box that appears. You may then perform the procedures explained in this chapter.

The setup for GroupWise 5 is very intuitive, using a lot of information that has been built into Windows 95. For example, GroupWise 5 can detect the type of modem installed on your computer.

You need to obtain most of the other setup information from your GroupWise system administrator. Once you have this information, configuring GroupWise Remote is a matter of completing some simple steps. Once the configuration is complete, you most likely won't need to change the settings unless your master system changes or you change your connection method.

TIP

It is a good idea to record your remote information, in case you need to re-enter it at a later date. Appendix D provides a worksheet for this purpose.

The first time you run GroupWise while not connected to the network, you will see the screen shown in Figure 9.1. This window displays a list of what needs to be set up so you can access your Remote Mailbox.

Once you click OK, you see the Remote Options dialog box. (To change your remote configurations later, you can access this screen by choosing Tools → Options and double-clicking the Remote icon.)

The GroupWise 5 Remote Options can be categorized into five areas: User Information, System Information, Connections, Time Zone, and Delete Options.

User Information

First, enter the user information in the top half of the dialog box, as shown in Figure 9.2.

F I G U R E 9 . 1 *GroupWise 5 Remote Introduction Screen*

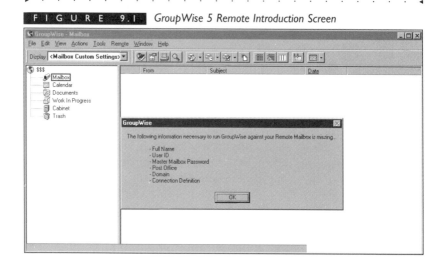

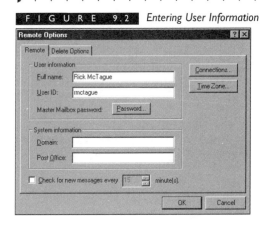

FIGURE 9.2 *Entering User Information*

Full Name

You must enter your complete name (first and last), which will help identify your messages.

TIP If you want the recipients of your messages to be able to tell when you have sent a message remotely, add (Remote) after your name. (Any text is valid on this line.)

User ID

This field requires your GroupWise User ID that was set up for you by the system administrator. It is not case-sensitive, but spelling definitely counts!

Master Mailbox Password

You must enter your Master Mailbox password in this field for remote access:

1. Click the Password button next to Master Mailbox password.

2. Type in the password, and confirm it by retyping the password.

3. Click OK.

This process completes the user information portion of setup.

System Information

Next, enter the system information in the bottom half of the dialog box, as shown in Figure 9.3. The information you enter in the fields for system information must be obtained from your system administrator. (Domains and post offices are logical divisions of your GroupWise system and are defined by the GroupWise system administrator.)

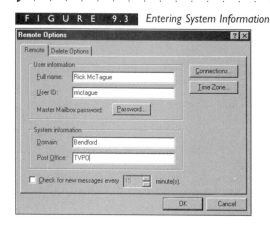

F I G U R E   9 . 3 *Entering System Information*

Domain

Type in the name of your GroupWise domain, provided to you by the system administrator.

Post Office

Type in the name of your GroupWise post office, provided to you by the system administrator.

If you are running GroupWise over the network, you can click Help → About GroupWise to view your UserID and Post Office.

TIP

Check for New Messages Every X Minutes

You can enter the interval that you want GroupWise to automatically connect to the master mailbox and update your remote system with new messages into the box labeled Check for new messages every *x* minutes.

This process completes the system information part of setup.

Connections

From the Remote Options screen, click on the Connections button to create connections to the master system. You will see the Connection Configuration dialog box shown in Figure 9.4. You must create at least one connection before you can start using GroupWise 5 Remote.

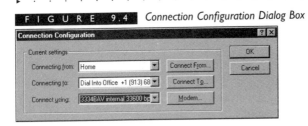

F I G U R E   9.4   *Connection Configuration Dialog Box*

If you want to return to this point later on (for example, to add, change, or delete connections), choose the Send/Retrieve option from the Remote menu and click the Configure button.

Connecting from

The Connecting from: field in the Connection Configuration dialog box is where you can create multiple remote profiles. For example, you can create a profile for getting remote messages from home or on the road (complete with a 9 before the area code and phone number, or with a PIN, for example).

Figure 9.5 shows the dialog box for creating a dialing from location. Select your location from the I am dialing from drop-down list, verify the location, and choose OK.

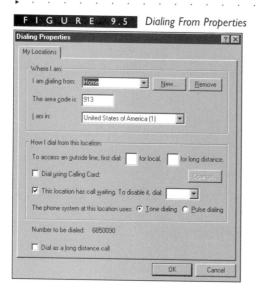

FIGURE 9.5 *Dialing From Properties*

Connecting to (Modem, Network, and TCP/IP)

In order to send and receive information while you are not connected to the network, you need to create a remote connection. Later, when you select the Connecting to: field in the Connection Configuration dialog box, you will be able to create, modify, or delete your connections, as shown in Figure 9.6.

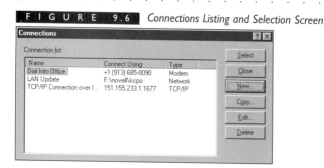

FIGURE 9.6 *Connections Listing and Selection Screen*

The connection you define determines how your computer will communicate with the GroupWise system. You can create as many connections as there are available in your GroupWise system. (Your system administrator will have connection information for you.) Some of the fields you complete might not make sense to you, but they are necessary to protect the security of the GroupWise system.

To create a new connection, click the New button from the Connections screen. As Figure 9.7 shows, there are three types of remote connections: Modem, Network, and TCP/IP. We discuss only the modem connection here, because the modem is by far the most common type of remote connection. We explain Network and TCP/IP connections toward the end of this chapter.

FIGURE 9.7 *Create Connection Dialog Box*

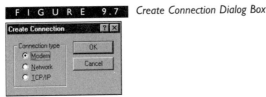

A modem connection is used to dial into the GroupWise Async gateway. The settings for this connection are determined by your system administrator. Figure 9.8 shows the Modem Connection dialog box.

FIGURE 9.8 *Modem Connection Dialog Box, General Settings*

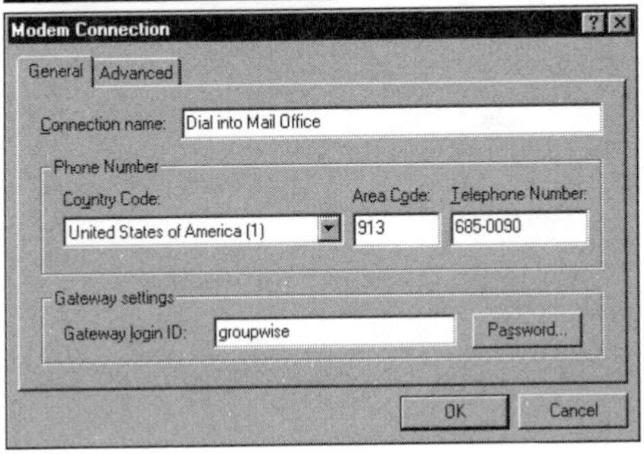

To create a modem connection:

1. Choose Modem from the Connections screen.

2. Enter a name for the connection in the Connection name: field, and enter the phone number in the Phone number: field.

TIP

Place a comma in the phone number field to signify a pause. For example, the following phone number dials an outside line, calls a calling card, pauses for 4 seconds, and enters a PIN number:

9,1-800-123-9999,,,,1111-22-333

NOTE

You won't need to include extra numbers to obtain an outside or long-distance line if you have created a Connecting from profile for your location. See "Connecting from" earlier in this chapter for more information.

3. The Gateway settings area is where you enter information needed to connect to the GroupWise Asynchronous gateway (a tech-y name for the computer that answers the phone when your computer calls in for messages). Enter the Gateway login ID, and click the Password button to enter the gateway's password. You will need to retype the password. (Remember, all passwords in GroupWise are case-sensitive.)

4. Click the Advanced tab to enter more information such as redial intervals, as shown in Figure 9.9.

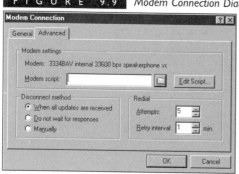

F I G U R E   9.9   *Modem Connection Dialog Box, Advanced Settings*

5. Enter the redial information (the number of attempts and how long to wait in between each attempt) — the defaults are usually sufficient.

6. Choose a disconnect method and optional modem script, and click OK to save the connection. All connection options all have one area in common: the disconnect method.

Selecting "When all updates are received" keeps the connection open until all responses have been received, after which the connection is terminated.

Selecting "Do not wait for responses" forces the disconnection as soon as requests are uploaded. You will see your responses the next time you connect.

Selecting "Manually" keeps the connection open until you click the Disconnect button.

Connect Using (Modem Selection)

The Connect using: portion of the Connection Configuration dialog box tells GroupWise Remote what device you will connect to the GroupWise system with. From this screen, you see a list of all available ports.

As you can see from Figure 9.10, all of the hardware ports installed in your computer will appear. Also notice that your installed modem in Windows 95 or Windows NT appears on the list; GroupWise Remote will use this modem.

F I G U R E   9 . 1 0   *Port Selection*

If you would like to configure the modem, click the Modem button. Notice that you can change the general modem properties, the connection preferences (only for the modem, not for GroupWise connections), and other dialing options, as shown in Figure 9.11.

Any alterations you make here will change the modem's properties in Windows 95, not just in GroupWise. The GroupWise program gives you a convenient way of accessing the Windows modem setup, instead of using Control Panel.

Once the three Connection Configuration settings have been specified—Connecting from:, Connecting to:, and Connect using:—click OK and the connection information will be saved in your Connections List. You are now ready to complete the next area of GroupWise Remote configuration, the Time Zone.

F I G U R E   9.11 *Modem Properties*

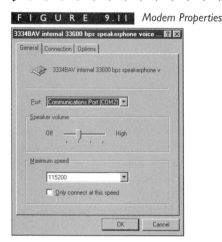

Time Zone

GroupWise needs to know the time zone where you reside so it can automatically adjust appointment times. This setting is important if you live in a time zone different than the time zone where your master GroupWise system is located.

GroupWise automatically adjusts the appointments you create depending on the Time Zone information that is entered here.

NOTE

To set your time zone, click the Time Zone button and choose the appropriate time zone from the list. As Figure 9.12 shows, the time zone for your computer is displayed graphically. Like your modem selection, the Time Zone setting should be automatically set by Windows 95.

F I G U R E   9 . 1 2 *Setting the Time Zone*

Delete Options

The Delete Options tab lets you configure the synchronization of deleted messages between your master and remote mailbox. The options at the top of the dialog box, as shown in Figure 9.13, let you specify what happens to messages in your master mailbox when you delete messages from your remote mailbox.

F I G U R E   9 . 1 3   *Remote Options, Delete Options tab*

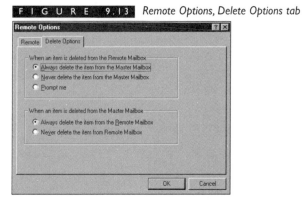

Always delete automatically deletes messages from your master mailbox when you exit from your remote mailbox; Never delete never deletes them. Prompt me asks you what to do with the master mailbox each time you delete a message from your remote mailbox.

The bottom half of the screen lets you configure what happens to your remote mailbox when messages are deleted from the master mailbox.

Using GroupWise in Remote Mode

There are very few functional differences between using GroupWise Remote and using GroupWise while logged into the network. The same set of program files are used, the screens all look the same, and you access all of your information the same way.

When you use GroupWise in the office (connected mode), you are working in your Master Mailbox, which is stored on the network. When you leave the office and need to use GroupWise, the program will use a remote version of your Mailbox, stored on your computer at home, or perhaps on your notebook computer. The messages and Calendar items you create in the Remote Mode are stored in the Remote Mailbox until you connect to the GroupWise system and synchronize the two Mailboxes.

Remember to connect after the last change you make to your Remote Mailbox. Otherwise, the master system will not be informed of the changes.

Remote Menu

One of the most noticeable differences about Remote Mode is a new menu, aptly called Remote. As you can see in Figure 9.14, there are five choices under the Remote menu:

▸ **Send/Retrieve:** Configure and initiate the remote connection here.

▸ **Retrieve Selected Items:** Retrieve the remaining portions of incomplete messages (because of item-request restrictions, such as when you retrieve subject lines only).

▸ **Pending Requests:** View and manage requests that are waiting to be uploaded and responded to by the master system. Usually, you won't need to do anything in this screen.

▸ **Connection Log:** View the connection details in the log file. You can also see this information if you click the Show Log button when you make a connection to the master system.

▶ **Disk Space Management:** This dialog enables you to manage the storage space used on your remote computer's hard drive by documents which are checked out or otherwise copied from GroupWise libraries. This was covered in detail in Chapter 8.

There is also a Remote icon added to the Options choice under the Tools menu where you can change your Remote configuration. See the "Configuring the GroupWise Client" section earlier in this chapter.

Sending Messages

For the most part, there is not much difference between using GroupWise remotely and using it on the network: You use the Address Book and send messages, create Calendar entries, and reply to and forward messages the same way. The only difference is that you need to connect to the master system to actually send messages. See the section titled "Connecting to the Master System" later in this chapter.

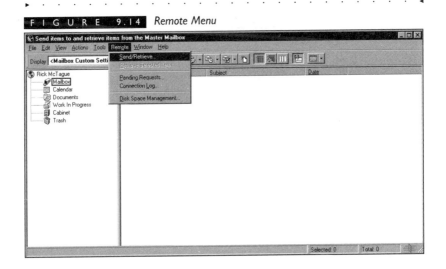

FIGURE 9.14 *Remote Menu*

Busy Search

Busy Search is slightly different if you are in Remote Mode. When you are creating an Appointment while you are out of the office, you may not want to wait until the Appointment request has been received (and either accepted or declined) by the people you need at the meeting. If you need faster information about whether they are available for an Appointment or not, set up Busy Search in the normal way. (See Chapter 6 for a complete discussion of Busy Search on the network).

Once you have configured the Appointment information for the Busy Search, choose to connect now or wait until the next time you connect to send the Busy Search request to the GroupWise system, as shown in Figure 9.15. Either way, you will receive the results of your Busy Search, and you can continue creating your Appointment request.

TIP

You should save the incomplete Appointment in the Work In Progress folder while you are waiting for the outcome of the Busy Search. When the results arrive, open the draft Appointment, complete the information, and choose Send. Don't forget to connect again to actually send the message to the system.

FIGURE 9.15 *Remote Busy Search Screen*

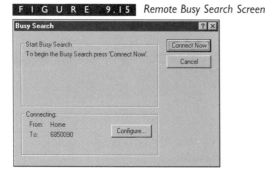

Proxy

The only feature you cannot utilize when you are using GroupWise Remote is the Proxy feature. Since the Proxy feature involves having access to someone else's Mailbox (and you are not logged into the network where the other user's Mailbox is), there is no way to use this feature.

Connecting to the Master System

GroupWise Remote Mode is a request-based system. A request-based system means that you work off-line reading messages, creating new Appointments, and making other changes to your Remote Mailbox. Once you have made all of your changes and are ready to connect to the main system, you will generate a list of requests for items.

One request will be to send out all of your outgoing messages. Another request will be to retrieve your new messages, sent to you since the last time you connected to the main GroupWise system. You can make other requests (for example, to get a new copy of the Address Book). When you connect using any of the methods listed in the previous section, your requests are transferred to the main GroupWise system.

The GroupWise system will generate responses to your requests, compress them, and transfer them via your connection to your Remote computer. Some of your requests will be handled in the same session that you sent them in (to get your new messages, for example), and others will be transferred the next time you connect.

Once the request list has been completed, the connection is terminated, and the responses are decompressed and added to your Remote Mailbox.

To request items:

1. Choose Remote → Send/Retrieve. The screen shown in Figure 9.16 appears.

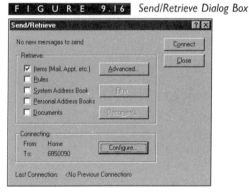

F I G U R E   9 . 1 6   *Send/Retrieve Dialog Box*

2. If you would like to change the request for items, click on the Advanced button to display the screen shown in Figure 9.17. Choose the options you want from the tabs:

   • On the *Retrieve* tab, you can configure the date range, which enables you to set the range of dates from which GroupWise will retrieve messages. The default is five days prior to the current day. If you have not connected in several days, you may need to increase this range. You can also choose Retrieve all changes since I last connected, which will set the range for you automatically.

- *Items* enables you to select what message categories you want to update (Mail and Phone, Appointments, and so on) and set up a filter to retrieve specific messages matching certain criteria, for example, messages that contain "Miller Project" in the subject. See Chapter 4 for a complete discussion of using filters.

- *Size Limits* will retrieve messages that fall into a particular size range. (For example, you may choose to only retrieve messages with attachments that are less than 30K in size.) You can also retrieve just the subject line, and then get the message information later. This feature can be very useful to minimize connection time and phone charges.

TIP

If after reading messages in the Mailbox you decide you need to see the complete message or attachment, choose Retrieve Selected Items from the Remote menu and connect in the normal way. The balance of the message content will be downloaded. You can use Ctrl-click to select more than one message, in order to save connection time.

- *Folders* enables you to select the folders you want updated. You can use this feature in conjunction with the Rules feature to move only those messages you want retrieved to a certain Remote folder, so you can simply download messages from this folder. The Folder feature makes the Remote connection more efficient. Simply click on the box next to the folder to select it for updating.

F I G U R E   9.17 *Configuring the Request for Items*

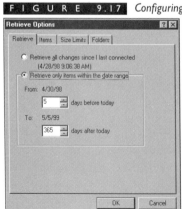

3. Click OK to return to the Send/Retrieve screen.

4. Make other selections from the Send/Retrieve screen as desired:

   • *Rules* will update all Rules between the Remote and Master Mailboxes.

   • *System Address Book* will update your Remote Mailbox with the most current Address Book. Click Filter to select which address book you want (your Post Office or Domain).

   • *Personal Address Book* will synchronize your Master and Remote personal address books.

   • *Documents* will enable you to select the documents you want to retrieve if you have GroupWise Document Management Services enabled on your system. You can select documents from their folders, and the documents will be transferred to your Mailbox. See Chapter 8 for more information about document management.

5. Verify that the connection you want to use appears at the bottom of the screen. If you need to change the connection, click on the Configure button and set up the desired connection. See "Connections" earlier in this chapter for more information.

6. Choose Connect to complete the request and connect to the master system.

The Connection Status screen appears, as shown in Figure 9.18.

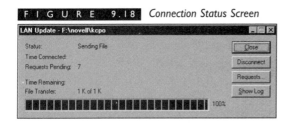

FIGURE   9.18 *Connection Status Screen*

To see the details of the connection, click the Show Log button. The Connection Log, shown in Figure 9.19, displays the session information and can be helpful in troubleshooting. This information is saved in a log file and can be accessed from the Connection Log option under the Remote menu.

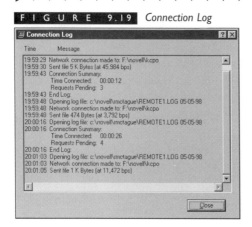

FIGURE 9.19 *Connection Log*

NOTE

It's a good idea to leave the computer alone while the connection is taking place. Any additional activity could slow the connection process or disrupt the link. During the connection activities, your computer is processing the new messages it just received, and you will see the dialog box shown in Figure 9.20.

FIGURE 9.20 *Updating Remote Mailbox*

Network and TCP/IP Connections

A network connection enables you to directly connect with your main GroupWise system through the network. This connection is used most often by people who travel to a branch office with a wide area network (WAN) link to the network.

All you need to know to use a network connection is the proper drive letter and a path to your GroupWise post office, as shown in Figure 9.21. Your system administrator should be able to provide you with this information.

Wise Guide: If you are using GroupWise on the network, among the information in the Help → About GroupWise box is the path (Drive letter and directory) of your post office. You can use this to enter the path in the network connection dialog box.

TIP

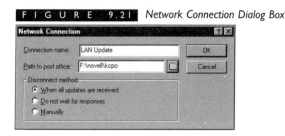

FIGURE 9.21 *Network Connection Dialog Box*

To create a network connection:

1. Choose Network from the Create Connection dialog box (shown earlier in Figure 9.7).

2. In the Network Connection dialog box, enter a name for the connection in the Connection name: field.

3. In the Path to post office: field, enter the drive letter and path to your post office.

4. Choose a disconnect method and then OK to save the connection.

A TCP/IP connection is very similar to the network connection. Instead of specifying the drive letter and path to your GroupWise post office, you specify the TCP/IP address of the post office server. Again, your system administrator can give you this information.

Wise Guide: If you are using GroupWise on the network with TCP/IP, among the information in the Help → About GroupWise box is the IP address and port number of your post office. You can use this to enter the path in the TCP/IP connection dialog box.

TIP

TCP/IP stands for Transmission Control Protocol/Internet Protocol. Basically, TCP/IP is a networking language that computers use to communicate. The Internet uses this protocol. A TCP/IP connection requires that the TCP/IP protocol be set up on your computer. In Windows 95, you can find out if TCP/IP is set up by following these steps:

1. From the Start button, choose Settings → Control Panel.

2. Double-click the Network icon.

3. Scroll down the list of items until you see TCP/IP --> NE2000 (instead of NE2000, you may see the name of your particular brand of network card, or you may see the words "Dial Up Adapter").

IMPORTANT

Don't change any of the settings in this or any other network screen unless your system administrator instructs you to do so.

If you don't have an entry for the TCP/IP protocol, you will need to add that protocol to your system to use a TCP/IP connection. (See your Windows 95 manual for instructions on how to do this, or contact your system administrator.)

To create a TCP/IP connection to your GroupWise post office:

1. Choose the TCP/IP button from the New Connection dialog box. The dialog box shown in Figure 9.22 appears.

FIGURE 9.22 *TCP/IP Connection Dialog Box*

TCP/IP Connection	? ☒
Connection name:	TCP/IP Connection over Internet	OK
IP Address:	151.155.233.1	Cancel
IP Port:	1677	
Disconnect method	
⦿ When all updates are received	
○ Do not wait for responses	
○ Manually	

2. Type in a name for the connection in the Connection name: field.

3. Enter the IP address of the post office server in the IP Address: field. (The address will be four numbers that are up to three digits each, separated by periods. See the example in Figure 9.22.)

4. Enter the port number in the IP Port: field. This number is usually 1677, but you can confirm this with your system administrator.

5. Choose a disconnect method and then OK to save the connection.

Hit the Road

One of the easiest features of GroupWise is also probably the most useful feature for Remote users. Hit the Road is a one-step way to update your Remote Mailbox before you leave the office.

While using GroupWise and connected to the network, as one of the preparations for your road trip, use the Hit the Road feature to do a last-minute synchronization of your Remote Mailbox and you are ready to go.

Wise Guide: If you use Hit the Road while connected to the network, a network connection is created automatically. You won't have to manually enter the network connection
TIP information discussed earlier.

To use Hit the Road:

1. While logged into GroupWise on the network, finish all messaging transactions (replies, new messages, and so on).

2. Choose Tools → Hit the Road. The dialog box shown in Figure 9.23 appears.

FIGURE 9.23 *'Hit the Road'Wizard Dialog Box*

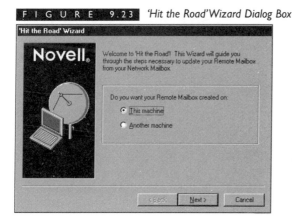

3. When prompted, enter the password for your mailbox in the dialog box.

You may see a message about needing to set a password on your Mailbox before you can use Hit the Road. The Security Options screen will appear. Enter a password (case-sensitive),
NOTE confirm it on the second line, and choose OK.

4. If a Remote Mailbox has never been created on this machine, you will be walked through setting it up on either this or another computer. If a Remote Mailbox has been set up previously, skip to Step 6.

5. Choose This machine and click Next. (If you choose Another machine, you can copy the setup file to a floppy disk. This choice should only be made by the system administrator.)

6. Enter the path to the Remote Mailbox. (Your system administrator may have a desired location, but you can choose anywhere you like on your C drive.) The default is C:\NOVELL\REMOTE. Click Next to move to the next screen.

7. In the GroupWise Async Gateways screen, shown in Figure 9.24, you will see a list of phone numbers for your remote computer to dial into. Your system administrator created these numbers for remote users to dial for the purpose of connecting to the main GroupWise system for updates. Select the appropriate number and click Next.

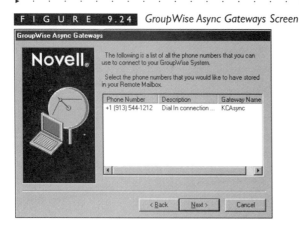

FIGURE 9.24 *GroupWise Async Gateways Screen*

8. Select which items you want to be updated to your Remote Mailbox this time by Hit the Road. You can configure the items each time you use Hit the Road, as shown in Figure 9.25.

FIGURE 9.25 *Update Items in Hit the Road*

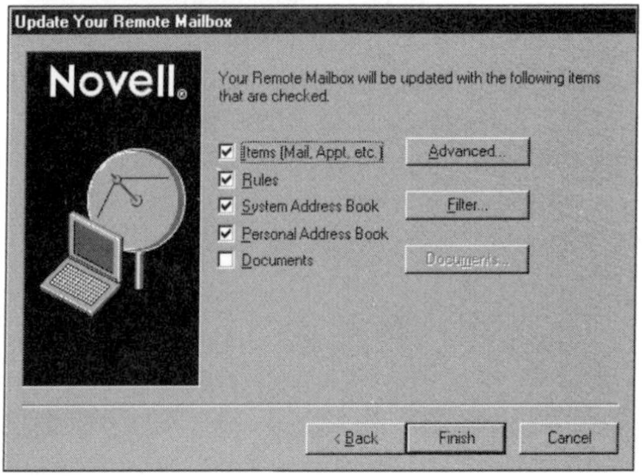

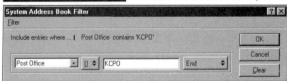

> If you would like to customize your items choices, click the Advanced button and make the appropriate selections.

NOTE

9. You can choose which address book you need to use by clicking the Filter button next to the System Address Book item. Select any of the items in the list to limit your Address Book as you like, as shown in Figure 9.26. (Chapter 4 includes a more complete discussion of the Filter box.)

FIGURE 9.26 *Remote Address Book Filter for Post Office Only*

System Address Book Filter		? X
Filter		
Include entries where ... ❚ Post Office contains 'KCPO'		OK
		Cancel
Post Office ▼ ▐ ◆ KCPO End ◆		Clear

10. If GroupWise Document Management is set up on your system, you can also select the documents you need by clicking the box next to Documents. You can then select the documents you need by clicking the Documents button and making your selection.

11. Click Finish. This action will initiate a network connection to your post office, and the items you selected will be downloaded into your Remote Mailbox.

Congratulations! You are now ready to Hit the Road.

IMPORTANT

You will see two or three extra windows open and close automatically while the synchronization takes place. If you want more information about what is happening, click the Show Log button of the Network Connection screen. While the update takes place, it is important to leave the mouse alone! Just let the process finish, and as long as there are no extra windows open that show connection activities, you can use the system.

Smart Docking

Suppose you are using a notebook computer and have been away on a business trip. When you come back into the office after using GroupWise Remote, any changes you have made while on the road since your last connection can be automatically updated to the network's master version of your Mailbox (your Master Mailbox). This feature is known as Smart Docking.

When you start GroupWise the first time after being off of the network, GroupWise automatically synchronizes the changes in your Remote Mailbox with your Master Mailbox. Because the connection type — modem or logged into the network — is sensed automatically, no configuration is necessary. The dialog box in Figure 9.27 shows what you will see.

FIGURE 9.27 *Remote Update Dialog Box*

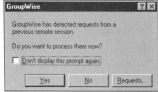

NOTE

If you select the Don't display this prompt again message, the Mailbox will be updated without any user intervention.

During the automatic mailbox update that takes place, you'll see Figure 9.28, which shows the Smart Docking Network Connection screen.

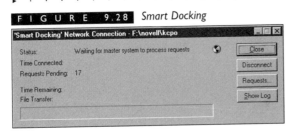

FIGURE 9.28 *Smart Docking*

With the Smart Docking feature of GroupWise, you don't need to worry about how you are connected to GroupWise, the program will keep your master mailbox synchronized with changes made in your remote mailbox. Of course, to get the updates from your master mailbox to your remote mailbox, the "Hit the Road" feature is used, as discussed earlier in this chapter.

Summary

GroupWise Remote enables mobile users to take their information with them, access it while they're gone, and update the GroupWise system when they get back. The ability to stay in touch with critical communications can make a big difference in today's fast-paced world.

CHAPTER 10

Customizing GroupWise

GroupWise enables you to customize your environment to reflect personal work style and preferences. In this chapter we explain the options for customizing your GroupWise environment.

Often, you can select options to override the defaults you set. For example, you may decide to set your default message priority level to Normal. When you need to send a high-priority message, you can change the priority level to High for that particular message (without changing the default). The next message you create will again use the default, Normal-priority level, unless you decide to override the default again.

In this chapter, we explain how to set GroupWise default options, how to customize the Toolbar, and how to customize your folders.

Setting Default Options

When you click Tools and then Options from the main GroupWise menu, you see the dialog box shown in Figure 10.1. Use this dialog box to set your GroupWise default options (in other words, your preferences).

FIGURE 10.1 *GroupWise Options Dialog Box*

You can set defaults for the GroupWise environment (that is, the overall program interface), for sending messages, for document management, for security, and for the Calendar.

NOTE The default settings for document management (the settings that correspond to the Documents icon in the Options dialog box) are explained in Chapter 8.

Environment Options

The Environment preferences group enables you to modify characteristics of the overall GroupWise program interface. When you double-click the Environment icon, you see a dialog box with five different tabs: General, Views, File Location, Cleanup, and Signature, as shown in Figure 10.2.

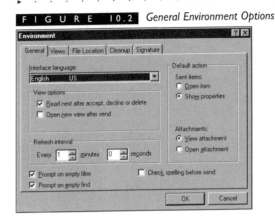

F I G U R E   1 0 . 2   *General Environment Options*

General

Under the General tab, you can set the following preferences:

▶ **Interface language:** The language you want to use in the client interface (menus, views, and so on). If the language you desire does not appear, contact your system administrator. Languages are enabled at the system level.

▶ **Refresh interval:** How often GroupWise checks for new messages (minimum is 1 minute, maximum is 60 minutes and 59 seconds, and the default is 1 minute).

▶ **Default action for Sent Items and Attachments:** Establishes what occurs when you double-click an item in your Sent Items folder or when you double-click a file attachment. For Sent Items, you can either open the message as it was sent, or view the properties (status information) about the message when you double-click it. For Attachments, you can either view the attachment using the GroupWise viewers or open the attachment with the associated application.

NOTE

After GroupWise is installed, when you double-click an item in the Sent Items folder or a file attachment, a dialog box appears asking you to set the default double-click option. These dialog boxes only appear once. After that, set the double-click action through Options, as explained earlier in this chapter.

▶ **Prompt on empty filter:** This option causes a message to appear if a filter you created does not allow any messages to appear.

▶ **Prompt on empty find:** This option causes a message to appear if a Find session doesn't generate any results.

▶ **Check spelling before send:** This option checks the spelling of each message (subject line and message body) when the Send or Post button is selected.

Views

Under the Views tab, you can set the following preferences, as shown in Figure 10.3:

▶ **Item type:** Select the category (Mail, Phone, Note, Appointment, Task, and Calendar) and the message type (Group or Personal) for which you want to set the default.

▶ **Views:** Choose from a list of available views for the selected item type.

▶ **Set Default View:** Highlight the view you want as the default for the item type you specify. When you choose File → New, this is the view that will appear for the message type you choose.

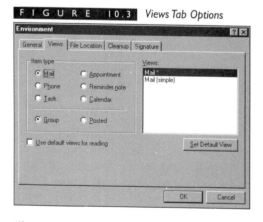

FIGURE 10.3 *Views Tab Options*

The Calendar default view is the view that appears when you select the Calendar View option from the Window menu.

NOTE

The Use default views for reading option enables you to read messages using your default views instead of the views they were sent with. For example, if someone sends you a Small Mail view message, you would normally see the message using the Small Mail view. If you marked the default views checkbox, you see the message in whichever view you chose as the default.

File Location

Figure 10.4 shows the preferences you can set under the File Location tab.

▶ **Archive directory:** The location of the parent directory of the actual archive directory that holds your archive message files. The system administrator may want you to place your archive files in a certain location.

▶ **Custom views:** The location for Custom View files. Custom views are specialized GroupWise views created with a view designer utility.

▶ **Save, check-out:** The default location for messages and attachments that you save, and the default location to place documents that you check out of a GroupWise library. (See Chapter 8 for more information on using GroupWise libraries.)

FIGURE 10.4 *File Location Tab Options*

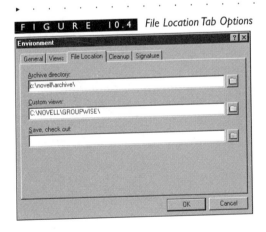

Cleanup

Figure 10.5 shows the preferences you can select under the Cleanup tab.

▶ **Mail and phone:** Specifies how old a phone or Mail message will be when it is automatically archived or deleted (minimum is 1 day, maximum is 250 days, and the default is Manual delete and archive).

► **Appointment, task, and reminder note:** Specifies how much past Calendar information you want to keep (minimum is 1 day, maximum is 250 days, and the default is Manual delete and archive).

► **Empty trash:** Specifies how long any deleted item will stay in the Trash folder (minimum is 1 day, maximum is 250 days, and the default is 7 days). Once messages have been emptied from the Trash folder, they are no longer retrievable.

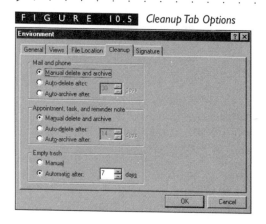

F I G U R E   I 0.5   *Cleanup Tab Options*

The options in Cleanup are performed when you start GroupWise. For example, if you have set Cleanup options so that messages are archived after 10 days, the archiving occurs when you start GroupWise on the tenth day after a message was received. The automatic Cleanup options can cause a slight delay when you start GroupWise.

Signature

You can enhance your messages with an Internet-style, custom signature. The signature can be added to the end of any message you send. You can include information such as a disclaimer, an encouraging quotation, or your phone number. GroupWise also lets you send your own personal information (name, phone numbers, and so on) as they appear in the Address Book in the new vCard format.

To configure a signature or vCard sending options, click the Signature tab in the Environment dialog box, as shown in Figure 10.6:

► **Electronic Business Card (vCard):** Enables the sharing of your personal information in the vCard format. vCard is a format for contact information that is recognized by many Internet-based and other types of e-mail systems. Sending a message with a vCard adds a .VCF file as an attachment. The recipient then opens the attachment and specifies which address book to add the contact into. For example, if you send a vCard attachment to a GroupWise recipient, the contact information is added to their personal address book or Frequent Contact list.

NOTE The information that you send when you include a vCard signature (i.e., attachment) is pulled from the GroupWise system Address Book, which is entered and created by the administrator.

▶ **Signature:** Type a signature in the Signature box as you want your signature to appear at the end of messages.

TIP You can copy text into the Clipboard from any application and place it in the Signature box. Graphics and other Rich Text Format (RTF) data cannot be used. Also, any text you enter will be preceded by two hard returns. This is helpful to know if you want your signature to appear with exactly one line between it and the last line of text in your message — in this case, don't end that last line with a hard return.

▶ **Automatically add:** Automatically adds the signature and/or vCard at the end of every message when you click Send.

▶ **Prompt before adding:** Asks you if you would like to add a signature and/or vCard information when you choose Send. This is the default option.

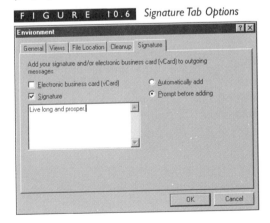

FIGURE 10.6 *Signature Tab Options*

Send Options

When you double-click the Send icon, you will see three tabs at the top of the Send Options dialog box: Send Options, Status Tracking, and Security as shown in Figure 10.7. Each tab contains customizable settings that affect the messages you send.

FIGURE 10.7 *The Send Options Dialog Box*

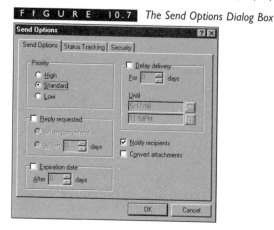

The Send Options tab affects all messages (e-mail, appointments, reminder notes, and tasks), as explained below:

- ▶ **Priority:** These options determine the default priority for each message type. High means the message appears with a red icon in the recipient's Mailbox, and may be delivered quicker by GroupWise. Standard means the message appears with a regular icon in the Mailbox. Low means the message appears with a dimmed icon in the Mailbox.

- ▶ **Reply Requested:** This option enables you to inform the recipient that you would like a reply to the message. When you set a Reply Requested option, GroupWise inserts text in the message body, stating that a reply is requested and how soon the reply is desired. The message icon shows two-way arrows, indicating that a reply is requested. When Convenient inserts `Reply Requested: When Convenient` in the message body; Within X Days inserts `Reply Requested: By mm/dd/yy` in the message body.

- ▶ **Expiration Date:** This option enables you to specify when the message will be automatically deleted from the recipient's Mailbox if the message is not opened.

▶ **Delay Delivery:** This option enables you to create a message now that will be sent after a specified number of days or on a certain date and time.

▶ **Notify Recipients:** This option specifies if the recipients receive a Notify message when the message arrives in their Mailboxes.

▶ **Convert Attachments:** This option specifies whether to convert attachments that are received through a gateway from another mail system. If the attachments are not converted, you will need the application with which the attachment was created to open it.

Status Tracking

Status tracking enables you to configure the amount of information available for each message you send, as shown in Figure 10.8:

▶ **Create a sent item to track information:** Specifies whether or not to create an entry in the Sent Items folder to track sent messages. Delivered shows you if and when the message was delivered to the recipient's Mailbox. Delivered and Opened shows you when the message was delivered and when the message was opened. All Information shows you all of the above information, plus information about when the message was deleted, accepted, declined, and so on. Auto Delete Sent Item automatically removes the message from your Sent Items folder after all recipients have deleted the item and emptied it from their Trash folders.

▶ **Return Notification:** Specifies action that will automatically happen when the recipient opens, accepts, deletes, or completes a message or calendar item. Mail Receipt means you receive a mail message in your mailbox informing you of the event. Notify means you receive an onscreen notification message informing you of the event. Notify and Mail means you receive both of the above.

Security

GroupWise includes support for programs that encrypt and digitally sign messages. The important thing to remember about message security is that the recipient must be able to understand and decrypt the message you sent. The default security options for all messages you send appear in Figure 10.9:

▶ **Conceal subject:** Prevents the message subject line from appearing in the recipient's Mailbox. The subject line only appears when the recipient opens the item. Use this feature as an additional security measure when prying eyes may obtain information simply by seeing the subject line in the Mailbox.

F I G U R E 1 0 . 8 *Status Tracking Options*

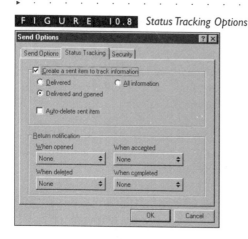

F I G U R E 1 0 . 9 *Security Options*

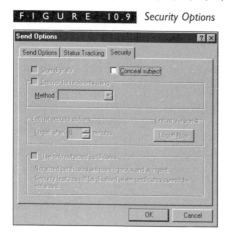

The single default option that comes with GroupWise "out of the box" is Conceal Subject. The other security options on the Security tab of Send Options enable you to configure the encryption and digital signatures of your messages (refer to Figure 10.9). These options are only available if you have previously installed an encryption program that is "GroupWise enabled."

Entrust Technologies, Inc. is one company who has created security solutions for desktop computing applications, such as GroupWise. If the Entrust security software is installed on your computer, the additional options on the Security tab of Send Options will be available. If not, they will be grayed out. More information on Entrust Technologies is available at: www.entrust.com.

NOTE As covered in Chapter 7, you can set message send options on a message-by-message basis. To set Send options for an individual message, open the message window, select File, and then choose Properties.

Security Options

When you double-click the safe icon in the Options dialog box, you see the Security Options dialog box. Unlike the Security option under the Send Options icon (which configures the encryption and digitally signs messages), the options available in the Security Options dialog box affect the security of your entire mailbox.

Password

One of the most important Security options is the Password option, shown in Figure 10.10.

To set a password on your mailbox:

1. Double-click the Security icon and click the Password tab once.

2. If you are changing a password, enter your old password in the Old Password field.

3. Type a password in the New Password field, and in the Confirm New Password field. Choose OK to set the password. The next time you start GroupWise, you must type in your password.

IMPORTANT The password is case-sensitive. Even though it can be reset by the administrator, be sure to record your password somewhere secure.

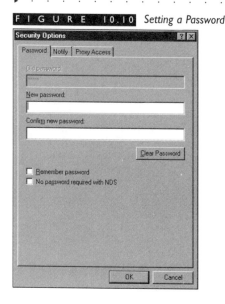

FIGURE 10.10 *Setting a Password*

IMPORTANT

Click the Remember password box if you don't want to enter your GroupWise password when you start GroupWise. If another person on the network tries to access your Mailbox, the person has to enter your password. As long as you are logged into the local machine as yourself, you won't have to type it in.

The No password required with NDS option will bypass the password screen when GroupWise is starting as long as you are logged into the network as a valid NDS user. This will probably be the case if you are using a NetWare-based network but might not be if you are using an NT-based network.

NOTE

This option does not change the GroupWise password if your network ID's password changes, it only bypasses the GroupWise password screen in certain cases as outlined. It also might be grayed out if your administrator has disabled this option.

Notify

The Notify tab enables you to use the Notify program, alerting you when you receive a message or when someone else receives a message. You can also be alerted by alarms set in your own Calendar as well as in other peoples'

Calendars. As with the Proxy feature, the other person needs to grant you the right to subscribe to notifications or subscribe to alarms. See the section titled "Using the Proxy Feature" in Chapter 7 for instructions on granting access to your Mailbox. The Notify tab options are shown in Figure 10.11.

FIGURE 10.11 *Notify Tab Options*

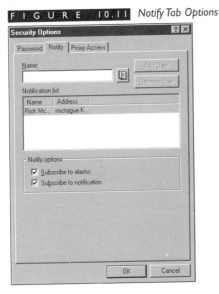

To receive notification when someone else receives a message (or to be alerted for another person's alarms):

1. Click the Address Book icon to the right of the Name field. Select a user from the list and choose OK.

2. With that person highlighted in the Notification List, check either the Subscribe to alarms or Subscribe to notification box. Notice that your name is already on the list.

3. Choose OK to apply your change. Your Notify program will now alert you for messages and/or alarms for both yourself and other users you selected.

Proxy Access

The Proxy Access is explained fully in Chapter 7.

Date Time Options

The Date & Time icon opens the Date Time Options dialog box, which contains three categories of options: Calendar, Busy Search, and Format.

Calendar

The Calendar options are shown in Figure 10.12:

▶ **Month Display Option:** First Day of Week enables you to specify which day you want to display as the first day of the week in your Monthly calendar view. Highlight Day visually distinguishes the selected days (such as weekends) on the monthly calendar view for quick viewing of the weekdays, for example. Show Week Number displays the number of the week on the left-hand side of the monthly calendar view.

▶ **Appointment Options:** Include Myself on New Appointments automatically adds your name as a recipient on any new meeting you create. Display Appointment Length (Duration) displays the length of time that the meeting will take up in hours and minutes. Display Appointment Length (End Date and Time) displays the date and time of the meeting. Default Appointment Length specifies the default duration of the appointment messages you send.

▶ **Work Schedule:** Start Time specifies the normal time your workday starts. End Time specifies the time your workday normally ends. Work Days specifies your scheduled work days.

TIP The Work Schedule will display a different setting when people use Busy Search to invite you for meetings. It also highlights the work days and times in the Week calendar view.

▶ **Line, Color Options:** These settings let you customize the appearance of appointments, reminder notes, and tasks in your calendar with lines and colors.

▶ **Alarm Options:** Use this option to configure whether to set an alarm when an appointment is accepted, and the default alarm interval.

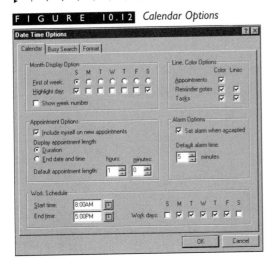

FIGURE 10.12 *Calendar Options*

Busy Search

The Busy Search options are shown in Figure 10.13:

▸ **Appointment length:** Specifies the default Appointment length for Appointments you create with the Busy Search feature.

▸ **Search range:** Enables you to specify the default number of days that you want to search.

▸ **From/To:** Enables you to specify the default time ranges during each day that you want searched.

▸ **Days to search:** Enables you to choose the default days you want included in the Busy Search.

Format

The Format tab options enable you to select your preferences for the display of dates and times, as shown in Figure 10.14:

▸ **System formats:** Enables you to set the default, system time format. This option enables you to access the Windows 95 Regional Settings dialog box.

▸ **General GroupWise format:** Enables you to specify a date and time display format that will be used as the default throughout GroupWise screens.

▶ **Specific GroupWise formats:** Enables you to specify different formats for the GroupWise main window, properties, and file information.

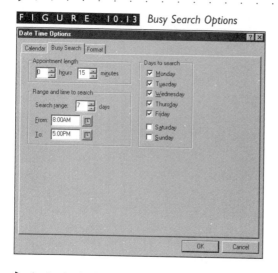

FIGURE 10.13 *Busy Search Options*

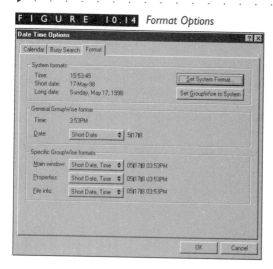

FIGURE 10.14 *Format Options*

Customizing the Toolbar

You can customize the Toolbar to include the functions and features you use most frequently, and you can arrange them in the order that makes most sense to you.

Toolbars appear in many different GroupWise screens. You have a Toolbar for each message view and for the main GroupWise screen. You can set different options for each.

To customize any Toolbar, right-click the Toolbar and select Properties. The Toolbar Properties dialog box appears, as shown in Figure 10.15.

The Show tab enables you to select what should be displayed on the Toolbar — only the picture or both picture and text. You can also specify one or multiple rows.

The Customize tab, shown in Figure 10.16, enables you to specify which GroupWise features appear on the Toolbar.

To add a menu option to the Toolbar:

► Click the category that the feature belongs to, for example, the Tools category contains options for the Address Book and Hit the Road tools.

► Double-click the button you want on the Toolbar. The button will appear on the Toolbar.

► Click and drag the button to your desired location on the Toolbar.

F I G U R E   10.15 *Toolbar Properties*

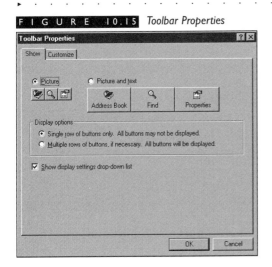

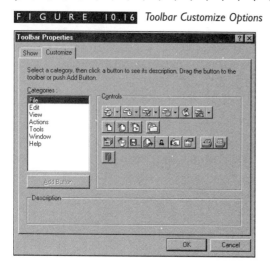

WiseGuide: When the Toolbar Properties dialog box is displayed, you can arrange the existing Toolbar buttons by clicking and dragging them to the desired locations.

NOTE

Customizing Your Folders

In Chapter 4, you see how to use folders to help organize your messages. By adjusting the properties of the folders in your Mailbox, you can arrange to see folder contents when the folder is opened, see who has access to the messages in the folder (if anyone), and specify what columns are displayed. Each folder can be customized individually. For example, the Mailbox can be set up to display only the Subject and From fields, and the Sent Items folder can be set up to display Subject, Opened status, and Date fields.

Property Sets

Even though you can set up a parent/child folder structure, folder properties are set for each folder individually. These folder properties are grouped into sets, as follows:

▸ **General:** Holds general information about the folder, such as the owner and description.

- **Display:** Configures folder settings to determine how messages are displayed in the folder and what columns are used.

- **Sharing:** Determines access to the messages in the folder.

The people who share a particular parent folder will not necessarily share the subfolders under the folder. Shared access to folders is set for the individual folder.

NOTE

The properties available for folders differ, depending on the folder you are configuring. All folders contain General and Display setting tabs. The Sent Items and Task List folders include a Find tab. The Trash folder contains a Cleanup property tab.

User-created folders contain a unique tab named Sharing. This tab enables you to share the folders with other GroupWise users.

To display or change the properties of a folder, right-click on the folder and choose Properties.

General

Figure 10.17 shows the General folder properties:

- **Type:** Describes the type of folder — Personal, Calendar, Mailbox, and so forth.

- **Owner:** Specifies the creator of the folder.

- **Contains:** Provides a summary of the folder's contents.

- **Description:** Gives a general description of the folder.

Display

Figure 10.18 depicts the Display tab of a personal folder. This setting configures the default display options. The Display drop-down list on the Toolbar lets you configure momentary display options, not default display properties. Every time the folder is accessed, the settings you make in the Display tab of the folder properties will be active.

WiseGuide: If you would like to save a custom set of folder settings, click the Save As button, enter a name for the folder setting, and choose OK. Your new custom set will appear under the Setting Name drop-down list.

NOTE

FIGURE 10.17 *General Folder Properties*

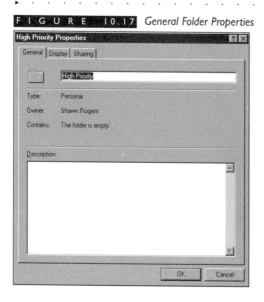

FIGURE 10.18 *Folder Display Properties*

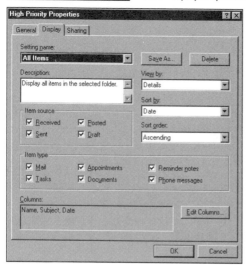

- **Setting name:** A drop-down list of preconfigured folder settings.

- **Description:** A description for this group of folder settings.

- **View by:** Sets the display to Message Details, Message Thread, or Calendar formats as the display for the items in this folder.

- **Sort by:** Determines a piece of information about the messages by which all messages in this folder will be sorted (for example, by Date, From, and so on).

- **Sort order:** Ascending or descending display of the items in this folder.

- **Item source:** Tells GroupWise what the originating source is of the messages in this folder — Received, Sent, Personal, or Draft messages.

- **Item type:** Specifies the types of messages contained in the folder — Mail, Appointments, Reminder Notes, Tasks, Documents, and Phone Messages.

- **Columns:** Determines which pieces of information will appear in the columns in the Items Area. Choose Edit Columns to add or delete columns.

TIP Make sure that the piece of information by which you are sorting the messages is also a column.

Sharing

Sharing options for folders determine who has access to the messages inside of them. Chapter 4 discusses how to use shared folders in detail.

Folder Content Display Options

This option changes which messages are displayed in a particular folder while the folder is opened, and is found in the drop-down list on the left side of Toolbar, as shown in Figure 10.19. Highlight a folder, click the down arrow next to the Display window on the Toolbar, and select the type of messages you want to be displayed, such as All Items or Received Items.

NOTE

This is only active for the moment the folder is opened and the choice is made. The next time the folder is opened, the default folder items will be displayed. These are configured in the properties of the folder, which was covered earlier in the "Customizing Your Folders" section.

F I G U R E   10.19   *Folder Content Display Options*

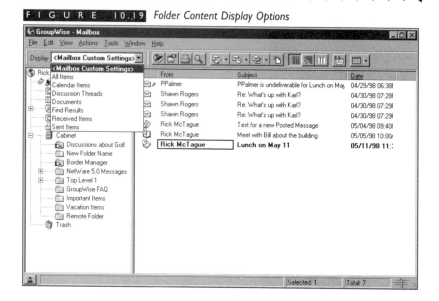

Show Appointment As

The Show Appointment As option lets you specify an appointment with different "busy properties." For example, when you create a new appointment, you can set it up as a "tentative" appointment that can be scheduled over, or set up a period of time (an appointment) as time "out of the office." People who perform a Busy Search will see the different types of appointments and have more information about your schedule than just "busy."

Free, Tentative, Busy, and Out of the Office are the four choices and are assigned to an existing appointment in the calendar. To set this option, highlight the appointment, choose Show Appointment As from the Actions menu, and select one of the four choices, as shown in Figure 10.20.

TIP

Right-clicking an appointment brings up a quick menu with this option on it.

► ◄

F I G U R E   1 0 . 2 0 *Show Appointment As Options*

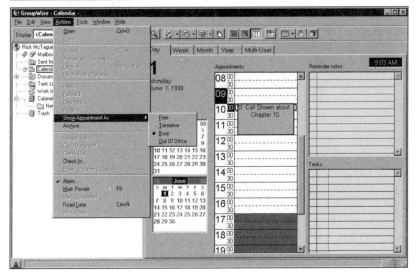

► ◄

Summary

In this chapter, we explained how to make GroupWise work the way you want it to by setting default GroupWise options, customizing your GroupWise Toolbars, and customizing your folders.

GroupWise Startup

The GroupWise Startup screen, shown in Figure A.1, is an introductory screen you see the first time you run the GroupWise client software. After installing the program, you normally don't see the Startup screen again. (When you double-click the GroupWise icon, GroupWise simply opens your mailbox.)

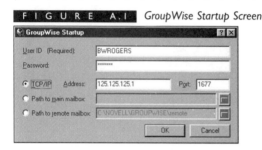

FIGURE A.1 *GroupWise Startup Screen*

Sometimes the GroupWise Startup screen appears if your GroupWise system does not recognize your login ID or GroupWise user ID. In such a situation, you are prompted to enter the startup information. The system requires this information in order to locate your stored GroupWise messages on the network.

If the Startup screen appears, the first thing to check is your GroupWise user ID and password. If the correct ID does not appear, type it in and choose OK.

If your user ID is correct, you will need to tell GroupWise how to locate your messages on the network.

Enabling GroupWise to Locate Your Messages

Depending on the configuration of your system, you will need to do one of the following:

- ▸ Provide a mapped drive to your GroupWise post office.
- ▸ Provide the TCP/IP information needed to connect to your Post Office Agent.

(The GroupWise post office is the database where your messages are stored on the network. The Post Office Agent is a program that handles communication between the GroupWise client program and your GroupWise post office.)

Using a Mapped Drive to the Post Office

If you use a mapped drive to connect to your post office, you must select the Path to Main mailbox option and enter the path, such as Y:\GWPOST. You should ask your system administrator whether you use a drive mapping and, if so, which path you should use.

Using a TCP/IP Connection to the Post Office

If you are using TCP/IP to connect to your post office in Client/Server mode, you must select the TCP/IP option and enter the required information to establish a TCP/IP connection to your post office.

The Address field requires the IP address of the Post Office Agent. This is NOT the IP address of your workstation. The Port field requires an IP port number. Again, you will need to ask your system administrator what information to enter. You could also ask another GroupWise user to check the Help → About GroupWise screen and tell you the IP address that appears in the dialog box. (Typically the port number is 1677.)

IMPORTANT To use a TCP/IP connection, your computer must be configured with TCP/IP. See your computer documentation for information on how to add TCP/IP to your workstation. Your system administrator will need to specify the TCP/IP address for your workstation.

Your system might not have Client/Server access enabled, in which case you would use the Network Post Office tab to configure a path to your post office.

Connecting to GroupWise

After you enable GroupWise to locate your messages by following the steps in the preceding section, you should be able to log in to your GroupWise system. Click OK.

You will notice a small screen telling you that you are connecting to GroupWise.

If GroupWise still cannot find your mailbox after you enter a network path or an IP address (usually as a result of a system failure), it will run in Remote Mode. You will still be able to use GroupWise off-line and will be able to send your messages when the system comes back online.

Calling Up the Startup Dialog Box

You can specify that GroupWise bring up the Startup screen every time it launches by simply adding a few characters to the GroupWise startup properties. Startup properties are parameters stored with the GroupWise icon that tell GroupWise what to do when it launches. Often, it is necessary to bring up the Startup screen when multiple users run GroupWise from the same computer.

To bring up the GroupWise Startup screen upon launching:

1. Right-click the GroupWise icon and choose Properties from the menu.

2. Click the Shortcut tab.

3. Place the cursor in the Target field and go to the end of the command.

4. Add a space, followed by **/@u-?**, after the GRPWISE.EXE command line. Be sure to include a space between the command line and the / character.

Figure A.2 shows the Properties screen with an example of the proper parameter syntax.

FIGURE A.2 *GroupWise Startup Properties Dialog Box*

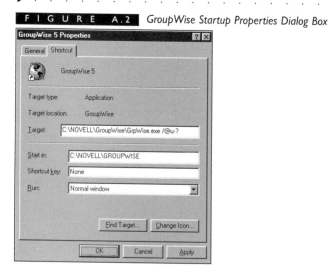

5. Choose OK. The next time you double-click the GroupWise icon, you will see the GroupWise Startup screen.

If you want to create multiple GroupWise icons, one for each person who uses the computer, follow the same steps listed previously, but substitute each user's GroupWise ID in place of the question mark in Step 4. (In Windows 95, you can copy an icon by right-clicking the icon and dragging it to a new location.) This permits several users to run GroupWise from a single machine; however, all users will share the same GroupWise default settings.

To allow multiple users on one machine to have different default settings in GroupWise, you must enable multiple user logins for Windows 95 by creating multiple user profiles. This is performed by using the Passwords option found in the Windows Control Panel. Refer to your Windows documentation for more information.

Online Help

If you have read the entire *Novell's GroupWise 5.5 User's Handbook* and are still uncertain as to how to perform a function in GroupWise, check the index at the back of the book for topics you may have missed. If you still can't find the answer, you should investigate the GroupWise online help system. This appendix explains how to use the online help resources available in GroupWise 5.5.

F1 Key

Press the F1 function key anywhere in GroupWise to get immediate help on the GroupWise feature you are using at that moment.

Help Button

In most dialog boxes, you will find a Help button. Click this button to view an in-depth explanation of the dialog box or feature you're using. The help information typically explains options and gives examples of how to use the dialog box.

Toolbar Help

If you allow the mouse pointer to rest for more than a second or two on any Toolbar button, a pop-up window appears, telling you what function the button performs.

Help Menu

The Help menu offers different options depending on the area of Group-Wise you're working in. For example, in the main GroupWise screen, the Help menu topics cover general GroupWise issues. If you have the Address Book open, the Help menu provides information about Address Book topics.

In the main GroupWise Screen, the Help Topics option under the Help menu opens the dialog box shown in Figure B.1. You can enter the first few letters of the topic you need help with, and the list will automatically scroll down to that topic.

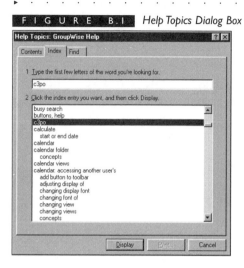

F I G U R E   B.1   *Help Topics Dialog Box*

When you have found the topic you want to learn more about, double-click the topic or click the Display button. If the Topics Found dialog box in Figure B.2 appears, you need to narrow your search. In the Topics Found dialog box, pick a topic you want to learn about and click the Display button.

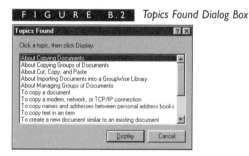

F I G U R E   B.2   *Topics Found Dialog Box*

GroupWise Guides

GroupWise Guides are built-in instructional aids that can help you perform certain tasks while GroupWise is running. Although you won't find a Guide for every possible task you can perform in GroupWise, these Guides come in handy when you are getting started with GroupWise.

Unlike some online help systems that simply explain procedures, Group-Wise Guides actually lead you through the necessary steps. For example, if you use a Guide to create an Appointment, the Guide will actually create the Appointment as it explains each step.

To access GroupWise Guides, select Help → Guides. There are five main areas of GroupWise Guides, as shown in Figure B.3:

- ▶ *GroupWise Basics* walks you through the most basic skills in GroupWise, such as setting up an appointment, retracting items, moving items to folders, and scheduling a recurring event. This guide also offers a "Move Up from GroupWise 4.1" topic that helps GroupWise 4 users transition to GroupWise 5.

- ▶ *Address Book* gives you a tour of the Address Book. This guide also walks you through the process of creating a Personal Group and adding a user to your personal address book.

- ▶ *Automating GroupWise* helps you create three rules with the Rules feature: one to handle messages while you're on vacation or away, another to sort mail, and the third to automatically update folders.

- ▶ *Sharing Your Work* teaches you how to share documents and folders, start a discussion group, and manage another GroupWise user's mailbox.

- ▶ *Managing Your Documents* takes you on a tour of a GroupWise document library, shows you how to create a new document or a new version of an existing document, and explains how to check out and check in a document.

Cool Solutions Web Magazine

The Cool Solutions Web Magazine option launches your Internet browser application (for example, Netscape Navigator) and takes you to the Web site at www.gwmag.com. GroupWise magazine is an online magazine that contains feature articles on how to improve your GroupWise productivity, as shown in Figure B.4.

GroupWise Guides

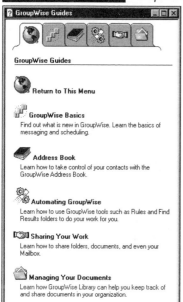

GroupWise Cool Solutions Web Magazine Home Page

Novell GroupWise Home Page

The Novell GroupWise Home Page option takes you to the Novell Group-Wise home page (`www.novell.com/groupwise`). The home page provides several helpful GroupWise links to find current information about GroupWise and other Novell products, along with a somewhat bizarre photo of a man holding a big clock in front of himself, as shown in Figure B.5.

FIGURE B.5 *GroupWise Home Page*

Tip of the Day

Tip of the Day lets you get just that — a tip of the day every time you launch GroupWise (if you select the Show Tips at Startup checkbox). See Figure B.6. We challenge you, however, to find something we didn't already teach you in this book.

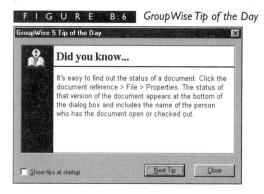

FIGURE   B.6   *GroupWise Tip of the Day*

About GroupWise

The About GroupWise option is helpful when you are troubleshooting in GroupWise. From this window you can determine which version of Group-Wise you're running, the release date, where you are running GroupWise from (your hard drive or the network), your user name, your file ID (an ID used to identify your Mailbox files on the network), the name of the GroupWise post office you are connected to, the path to the post office (if you are using a drive-mapped connection), and the IP address you are using to connect to the post office (if you are running in Client/Server mode).

Internet Features

You can use GroupWise to send and receive e-mail over the Internet, as long as the proper groundwork has been put in place. The groundwork involves configuring your GroupWise system's link to the Internet so messages can pass to and from the Internet. Your GroupWise system administrator should handle this configuration.

For the purposes of this appendix, assume that your GroupWise system has been configured with the following:

- ▸ A connection to the Internet

- ▸ A registered Internet address for your company (for example, shicktools.com)

- ▸ A GroupWise domain named INTERNET (a *domain* is the part of your GroupWise system that handles the administration of messages)

- ▸ A gateway, known as the GroupWise Internet Agent, to transfer messages to and from the Internet

You can use GroupWise to send e-mail messages over the Internet to anyone with an Internet connection, including users who have accounts with Internet Service Providers (ISPs) and people at other companies who use different e-mail systems.

Because the messages in GroupWise are formatted in a way that is unique to GroupWise, your messages must be translated into a universal format before they can be sent over the Internet. This common format is called Simple Mail Transfer Protocol (SMTP).

Remember that not all of the GroupWise message types will be understood or supported by the receiving e-mail system. For example, if you send an Appointment to someone who does not have GroupWise, that person will receive the message as a regular e-mail message.

Addressing Internet Mail

The GroupWise addresses you use for Internet e-mail must be converted to the proper format before your messages can be delivered to people over the Internet.

A standard Internet e-mail address has the following format:

user@domain.com

The user portion of the address refers to the individual to which you are sending e-mail. The domain.com portion refers to the registered Internet domain name for the person's company or ISP. (Other types of Internet addresses have different extensions at the end, such as .org or .edu.)

Here is an example of an Internet e-mail address:

rmctague@shicktools.com

Once you know the Internet address of the person you want to communicate with, you need to use the proper GroupWise Internet address format.

In our example, the system administrator has set up a domain named INTERNET. From our GroupWise system, we simply open up a new Mail message and place the address in the To field like this:

INTERNET:rmctague@shicktools.com

When the message is sent, GroupWise sends the message to the proper GroupWise domain through a GroupWise Internet Agent, and uses the rmctague@shicktools.com portion of the address to route the message over the Internet.

NOTE   Your system administrator might use GroupWise addressing rules to eliminate the need for the text that precedes the actual Internet address. If you don't know how to address messages to the Internet, ask your administrator for instructions.

You can store people's Internet addresses in a personal address book. (See Chapter 3 for more information about personal address books.)

Embedding Internet Elements in Messages

GroupWise enables you to embed Internet elements within your messages automatically. Suppose you are surfing the Web and you run across a site that you know a friend would appreciate. With GroupWise 5, you simply enter that site's Uniform Resource Locator (URL) in the message subject line or the message body and the URL automatically becomes a link to the Web site within the recipient's message.

Figure C.1 shows an e-mail message that has an embedded URL in the subject line and an embedded e-mail address in the message body.

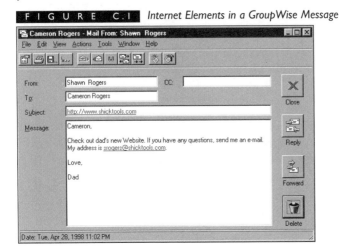

FIGURE C.1 *Internet Elements in a GroupWise Message*

If the recipient clicks the embedded Internet address, a new message opens and is automatically addressed to that address. If the recipient clicks the URL, the recipient's Web browser launches and that Web site opens.

TIP If you include a URL in the subject line, the recipient can go directly to the Web site by clicking the URL Subject line from the main GroupWise window.

GroupWise Remote Mode Worksheet

Use this worksheet to record the configuration information needed to set up GroupWise in Remote Mode. If you have any questions about the terms used in this table, see Chapter 10.

User Information

Record your User Information when configuring Hit the Road (Tools → Hit the Road), or GroupWise in Remote Mode (Tools → Options → Remote):

Full Name: _____

User ID:_____

Master Mailbox Password: _____

System Information

Record the GroupWise System Information when configuring Hit the Road, or GroupWise in Remote Mode. This information usually comes from the system administrator:

Domain: _____

Post Office: _____

GroupWise Connections

The next three items are for recording information about different types of connections to the main GroupWise system. This information is usually provided by the system administrator. While running GroupWise in Remote Mode, click Tools → Options → Remote and click the Connections button on the Remote tab to create and edit connection information.

Network Connection Configuration

Connection Name: _____

Path to Post Office: _____

TCP/IP Connection Configuration

Connection Name: _____

TCP/IP Address of GroupWise Mail Server: _____

IP Port Number of GroupWise Mail Server:_____

Modem Connection Configuration

Connection Name: _____

Gateway Login ID: _____

Gateway Login ID Password: _____

Time Zone

Enter your time zone here:

Time Zone: _____

GroupWise 5
WebAccess Client

The WebAccess version of the GroupWise client enables you to access your GroupWise mailbox from your Web browser, no matter where you happen to be in the world. With WebAccess, you can check your send new GroupWise messages, process incoming messages, check your calendar, schedule appointments, send tasks, and more. You can use WebAccess to do almost all of the GroupWise tasks you would do from regular GroupWise.

IMPORTANT The GroupWise system must be properly configured before you can access your mailbox from your Web browser. Ask your system administrator if your GroupWise system supports WebAccess.

GroupWise 5.5 WebAccess comes in three versions: the regular version, the Java-enabled version, and the "no-frames" version. If your machine has the power and your browser supports Java, you should use the Java version. For underpowered machines or nonstandard browsers, use the regular WebAccess version. For severely underpowered computers or for very slow Internet connections, use the no-frames version.

NOTE The screen shots in this appendix show the Java-enabled version.

Running WebAccess

To run the WebAccess GroupWise client, simply launch your Web browser and go to the URL established for WebAccess. The correct URL depends on how your administrator has set up the system (for example, at Novell you go to `gmail.novell.com`). Ask your administrator for the URL you should use. When you access your WebAccess address, you will encounter the login screen, shown in Figure E.1.

Enter your GroupWise user ID and your mailbox password (which is required), select the version of GroupWise WebAccess you want to use, and then click the Login button.

The WebAccess main screen, shown in Figure E.2, appears automatically. You can access all of the messaging features of GroupWise from the main screen.

FIGURE E.1
WebAccess Client Login Screen

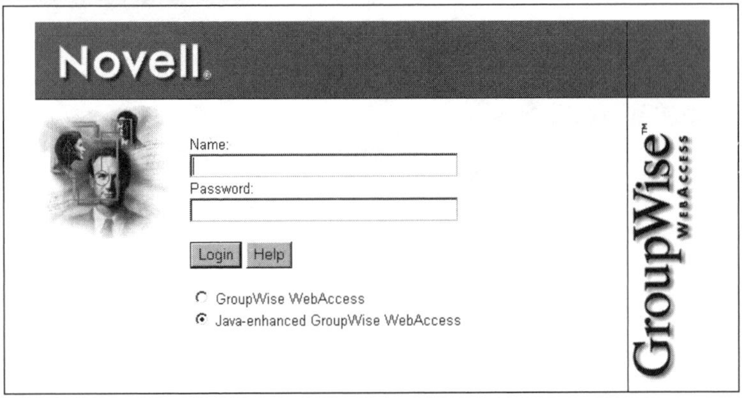

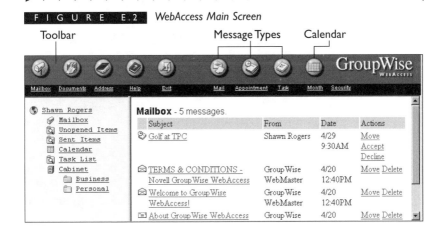

FIGURE E.2 WebAccess Main Screen

The GroupWise WebAccess client functions like a regular Web page. To read a mail message, simply click your mouse on the message in your mailbox. A typical mail message is shown in Figure E.3.

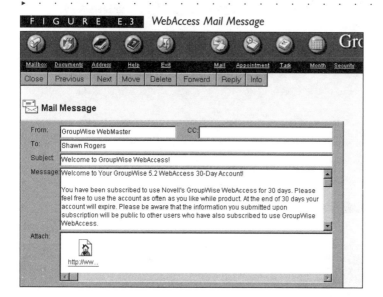

FIGURE E.3 *WebAccess Mail Message*

Notice that the typical mail message actions are available on the Toolbar located just above the message. The Java-enhanced version shows file attachments in an attachment window. The regular version of WebAccess displays the message as simple text.

Because using the GroupWise WebAccess client is very intuitive if you've used the regular GroupWise client (and read this book), we won't kill any more trees to document all of the messaging features. We'll just show you how to send an e-mail message to help you get oriented, and then we'll show you some of the few features that are significantly different from the regular GroupWise client.

Sending Messages

Sending messages from the WebAccess client is as simple as reading them. Each of the message types is available at the top of the main WebAccess screen. A WebAccess mail message screen is shown in Figure E.4. Enter each field just as you would when using another version of the GroupWise client, and click Send when you're done.

TIP Novell recommends that you attach files to messages just *before* you send the message. In other words, don't attach files until after you have completed all message fields and after you've used the spell checker.

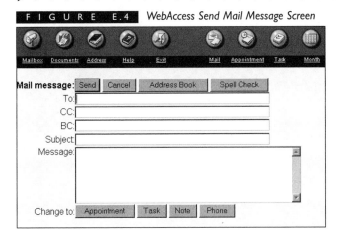

FIGURE E.4 *WebAccess Send Mail Message Screen*

Using the Spell Checker

The WebAccess client's spell checker is a Java applet; therefore, to spell-check your messages you must be using the Java version of WebAccess. The spell-checking applet is shown in Figure E.5. To run the spell checking applet, simply click the Spell Check button after you have finished typing your message.

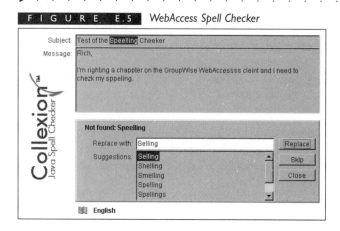

FIGURE E.5 *WebAccess Spell Checker*

Using the Address Book

The WebAccess Address Book interface is a bit different than that of the regular GroupWise client. The Java-enhanced Address Book is shown in Figure E.6.

FIGURE E.6 *WebAccess Address Book*

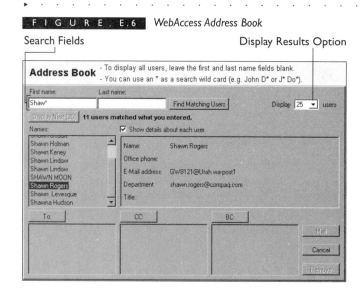

Search Fields

Display Results Option

To find names in the Address Book, just click the Address button on the toolbar or click the Address Book button at the top of a mail message you are writing.

To view all names in the Address Book, leave the name fields empty and click the Find Matching Users button. By default, the Address Book displays only 25 names at a time, so using this method could get tedious because you have to wait for the results of each address lookup to load from the Web server.

TIP You can specify that more names appear after each search by clicking the Display Users drop-down box and choosing a higher value. However, this will increase the time it takes to download the results of each search.

To narrow down your search, use the asterisk (*) wildcard, such as **J*** in the First Name field and **Do*** in the Last name field to find all people with first names beginning with *J* and last names beginning with *Do*. When you locate the name you want, click the To, CC, or BC fields to enter the name, and then click OK to close.

Summary

This should be enough to get you started with the WebAccess version of the GroupWise client. If you need more assistance with the WebAccess client, help is just a click away from the Help button on the main screen. Remember, some of the WebAccess features are dependent upon the Web browser you are using. If a feature doesn't appear to work or is not available, check the Help resource to verify that the feature is supported by your browser.

*I*ndex

sharing property, searching for documents by, 160
Sharing Your Work guide, 230
Show Appointment As options, 218–219
Show tab, Toolbar Properties dialog box, 213
signature option, typing information for into Signature box, 202
Signature tab, Environment dialog box, 202
Simple Mail view, versus Mail view, 21–22
Simple Mail Transfer Protocol (SMTP) format, 236
Smart Docking, 194–195
Specific GroupWise formats option, Date Time Options dialog box, 210
starting GroupWise, 2, 223–225
Startup dialog box, calling up, 224–225
Startup Properties dialog box, bringing up upon launching GroupWise, 224–225
status, searching for documents by, 160
status messages, 73–75
  descriptions of, 73
  message type/status correspondence chart, 74
status-tracking options, 131
  applying to a message you are creating, 129
Status Tracking tab, Send Options dialog box, 205
subject property, searching for documents by, 159
summary area, GroupWise main screen, 3–4
System Address Book Filter dialog box, 193
system address books, 34, 35
System formats option, Date Time Options dialog box, 211
system information, entering in Remote Options dialog box, 174

T

Task List folder, Folders List, 7–8, 88, 89
task management, and group calendaring, 98–115
Task messages
  addressing, 103
  delegating or assigning tasks with, 20
  setting priority codes for, 103–104
Task view, Calendar, 87

Tasks
  accepting, 106–107
  declining, 107
  delegating, 107
  granting access to with Proxy feature, 124
  marking private, 132
  monitoring, 105
  receiving, 106–107
  rescheduling, 93–94
  retracting, 105
  sending, 102–104
  valid priority codes, 103
TCP/IP connection, using to the post office, 223
TCP/IP connection, Remote Mode, 168
  checking for in Windows 95, 190
  creating a connection to your GroupWise post office, 189–190
TCP/IP Connection dialog box, 190
TCP/IP settings, configuring in Startup screen, 2
time-management features, GroupWise, 80–95
Time Zone, setting, 180
Tip of the Day, 232–233
To:, CC:, and BC: fields, GroupWise Address Book, 35
Toolbar, GroupWise main screen, 3, 11
  adding a menu option to, 213
  Create New Mail icon on, 19
Toolbar help, 228
Toolbar Properties dialog box, customizing the toolbar in, 213–214
Tools ➪ Busy Search command, performing a search before creating an Appointment message, 102
Tools menu, using the Find option in, 50–53
Tools ➪ Options command, changing Busy Search defaults with, 102
Topics Found dialog box, 229
Trash folder, Folders List, 9–10
  managing, 77
  purging messages from, 31
  restoring messages from, 31

U

unarchiving messages, 55
undeleting, e-mail messages, 31

my2cents.idgbooks.com